S0-BON-594

WEST BEND LIBRARY

Privacy

Other Books of Related Interest:

Opposing Viewpoints Series

Censorship

Gays in the Military

Human Rights

The U.S. Intelligence Community

Current Controversies Series

Teens and Privacy

At Issue Series

Are Social Networking Sites Harmful?

Should the Internet Be Free?

Sexting

The Right to Die

"Congress shall make no law . . . abridging the freedom of speech, or of the press."

First Amendment to the U.S. Constitution

The basic foundation of our democracy is the First Amendment guarantee of freedom of expression. The Opposing Viewpoints Series is dedicated to the concept of this basic freedom and the idea that it is more important to practice it than to enshrine it.

OPPOSING VIEWPOINTS® SERIES

| Privacy

Roman Espejo, Book Editor

GREENHAVEN PRESS
A part of Gale, Cengage Learning

GALE
CENGAGE Learning™

Detroit • New York • San Francisco • New Haven, Conn • Waterville, Maine • London

WEST BEND LIBRARY

Christine Nasso, *Publisher*
Elizabeth Des Chenes, *Managing Editor*

© 2011 Greenhaven Press, a part of Gale, Cengage Learning

Gale and Greenhaven Press are registered trademarks used herein under license.

For more information, contact:
Greenhaven Press
27500 Drake Rd.
Farmington Hills, MI 48331-3535
Or you can visit our Internet site at gale.cengage.com

ALL RIGHTS RESERVED.
No part of this work covered by the copyright herein may be reproduced, transmitted, stored, or used in any form or by any means graphic, electronic, or mechanical, including but not limited to photocopying, recording, scanning, digitizing, taping, Web distribution, information networks, or information storage and retrieval systems, except as permitted under Section 107 or 108 of the 1976 United States Copyright Act, without the prior written permission of the publisher.

For product information and technology assistance, contact us at

Gale Customer Support, 1-800-877-4253
For permission to use material from this text or product, submit all requests online at
www.cengage.com/permissions

Further permissions questions can be emailed to permissionrequest@cengage.com

Articles in Greenhaven Press anthologies are often edited for length to meet page requirements. In addition, original titles of these works are changed to clearly present the main thesis and to explicitly indicate the author's opinion. Every effort is made to ensure that Greenhaven Press accurately reflects the original intent of the authors. Every effort has been made to trace the owners of copyrighted material.

Cover image copyright Flying Colours Ltd/Digital Vision/Getty Images.

LIBRARY OF CONGRESS CATALOGING-IN-PUBLICATION DATA

Privacy / Roman Espejo, book editor.
    p. cm. -- (Opposing viewpoints)
    Includes bibliographical references and index.
    ISBN 978-0-7377-4984-7 (hardcover) -- ISBN 978-0-7377-4985-4 (pbk.)
    1. Privacy, Right of--United States. I. Espejo, Roman, 1977-
    JC596.2.U5P755 2010
    323.44'80973--dc22
                                                    2010014222

Printed in the United States of America
1 2 3 4 5 6 7 14 13 12 11 10

Contents

YA
323.448
P93

Chapter 3: Is Medical Privacy Adequately Protected?

Chapter 4: How Should Privacy Be Protected?

Why Consider Opposing Viewpoints?

> "The only way in which a human being can make some approach to knowing the whole of a subject is by hearing what can be said about it by persons of every variety of opinion and studying all modes in which it can be looked at by every character of mind. No wise man ever acquired his wisdom in any mode but this."
>
> *John Stuart Mill*

In our media-intensive culture it is not difficult to find differing opinions. Thousands of newspapers and magazines and dozens of radio and television talk shows resound with differing points of view. The difficulty lies in deciding which opinion to agree with and which "experts" seem the most credible. The more inundated we become with differing opinions and claims, the more essential it is to hone critical reading and thinking skills to evaluate these ideas. Opposing Viewpoints books address this problem directly by presenting stimulating debates that can be used to enhance and teach these skills. The varied opinions contained in each book examine many different aspects of a single issue. While examining these conveniently edited opposing views, readers can develop critical thinking skills such as the ability to compare and contrast authors' credibility, facts, argumentation styles, use of persuasive techniques, and other stylistic tools. In short, the Opposing Viewpoints Series is an ideal way to attain the higher-level thinking and reading skills so essential in a culture of diverse and contradictory opinions.

In addition to providing a tool for critical thinking, Opposing Viewpoints books challenge readers to question their own strongly held opinions and assumptions. Most people form their opinions on the basis of upbringing, peer pressure, and personal, cultural, or professional bias. By reading carefully balanced opposing views, readers must directly confront new ideas as well as the opinions of those with whom they disagree. This is not to argue simplistically that everyone who reads opposing views will—or should—change his or her opinion. Instead, the series enhances readers' understanding of their own views by encouraging confrontation with opposing ideas. Careful examination of others' views can lead to the readers' understanding of the logical inconsistencies in their own opinions, perspective on why they hold an opinion, and the consideration of the possibility that their opinion requires further evaluation.

Evaluating Other Opinions

To ensure that this type of examination occurs, Opposing Viewpoints books present all types of opinions. Prominent spokespeople on different sides of each issue as well as well-known professionals from many disciplines challenge the reader. An additional goal of the series is to provide a forum for other, less known, or even unpopular viewpoints. The opinion of an ordinary person who has had to make the decision to cut off life support from a terminally ill relative, for example, may be just as valuable and provide just as much insight as a medical ethicist's professional opinion. The editors have two additional purposes in including these less known views. One, the editors encourage readers to respect others' opinions—even when not enhanced by professional credibility. It is only by reading or listening to and objectively evaluating others' ideas that one can determine whether they are worthy of consideration. Two, the inclusion of such viewpoints encourages the important critical thinking skill of objectively evaluating an author's credentials and bias. This evaluation will illuminate an author's reasons for taking a particular stance on an issue and will aid in readers' evaluation of the author's ideas.

It is our hope that these books will give readers a deeper understanding of the issues debated and an appreciation of the complexity of even seemingly simple issues when good and honest people disagree. This awareness is particularly important in a democratic society such as ours in which people enter into public debate to determine the common good. Those with whom one disagrees should not be regarded as enemies but rather as people whose views deserve careful examination and may shed light on one's own.

Thomas Jefferson once said that "difference of opinion leads to inquiry, and inquiry to truth." Jefferson, a broadly educated man, argued that "if a nation expects to be ignorant and free . . . it expects what never was and never will be." As individuals and as a nation, it is imperative that we consider the opinions of others and examine them with skill and discernment. The Opposing Viewpoints Series is intended to help readers achieve this goal.

David L. Bender and Bruno Leone,
Founders

Introduction

> "Making connections—finding people you know, learning about people, searching for what people are saying about topics that interest you—is at the core of our product. This can only happen when people make their information available and choose to share more openly."[1]
>
> —Facebook,
> "A Guide to Privacy on Facebook"

> "These companies will never stop trying to chip away at our information. Their entire business model is based on the notion of 'monetizing' our privacy. To succeed they must slowly change the notion of privacy itself—the 'social norm,' as Facebook puts it—so that what we're giving up doesn't seem so valuable."[2]
>
> —David Lyons,
> Newsweek, February 17, 2010

At East Stroudsburg University (ESU) in Pennsylvania, sociology professor Gloria Gadsden was placed on administrative leave after her frustrated status updates on Facebook, a social-networking site, inexplicably found their way to her students. On January 21, 2010, she wrote, "Does anyone know where to find a very discreet hitman? Yes, it's been that kind of day ..." Several weeks later, Gadsden ruminated that she "had a good day today, DIDN'T want to kill even one student:-). Now Friday was a different story." A change in

1. http://www.facebook.com/privacy/explanation.php.
2. http://www.newsweek.com/id/233773.

Facebook privacy settings allowed students listed in her "friends" to read them, although Gadsden thought she had restricted them. "I actually did see that page as something that was not a part of ESU, not a part of my professional life," she told *USA Today*. "I don't invite students into that part of my life."[3]

Gadsden's experience demonstrates that Facebook users may be unaware of how the privacy settings work or when they change. In fact, its privacy settings and policies have been recently fine-tuned to address such confusion. In December 2009, the social-networking site did away with the "regional networks" privacy setting, which opened the possibility for a user to unintentionally make his or her information available to areas as large as cities and countries. Facebook also, for the first time, enabled users to control who can see an individual post or status update. Many welcomed these efforts. "We're glad to see Facebook finally put privacy front and center for every one of its users,"[4] stated Nicole Ozer, technology and civil liberties policy director of the American Civil Liberties Union of Northern California.

However, an accompanying change in the Facebook privacy settings concerned some critics. The privacy "transition tool," which aids in configuration, recommended default settings that widen the accessibility of user status updates and posts from "Your Network and Friends" to virtually anyone on the Internet. The "Facebook privacy transition tool is clearly designed to push users to share much more of their Facebook info with everyone, a worrisome development that will likely cause a major shift in privacy level for most of Facebook's users, whether intentionally or inadvertently,"[5] said Kevin Bank-

3. *USA Today*, March 2, 2010. www.usatoday.com/news/education/2010-03-02-facebook-professors_N.htm.

4. *Bytes and Pieces*, December 9, 2009. www.aclunc.org/issues/technology/blog/facebook_privacy_in_transition_-_but_where_is_it_heading.shtml.

5. www.eff.org, December 9, 2009. http://www.eff.org/deeplinks/2009/12/facebooks-new-privacy-changes-good-bad-and-ugly.

ston, senior staff attorney with the Electronic Freedom Foundation. Ozer also believes that the change is counterproductive. "We are concerned that the transition tool and other changes actually discourage or eliminate some privacy protections that Facebook users currently employ."[6]

That December, another change to the visibility of information on Facebook really worried Bankston. Lists of friends, networks and pages a member is a "fan" of became treated as "publicly available information" without an option to keep them private. Bankston alleged that this seemingly innocuous policy can have real-life repercussions upon privacy. "For example, you might want to join the fan page of a controversial issue (like a page that supports or condemns the legalization of gay marriage), and let all your personal friends see this on your profile, but hide it from your officemates, relatives or the public at large," he stated.

In February 2010, Facebook announced a rehaul of its privacy settings once again; this time, users were given control of how their information is shared through applications, Facebook's, as a well as third parties'. "There are now granular privacy options that enable you to personalize the audience for each piece of content you share through applications," the company blogged. "For example, maybe you don't want all of your friends to see the humorous greeting card you just posted from an application. Now you can set that post to be viewable only by certain friends."[7]

The ongoing changes in Facebook's privacy settings show how social media and emerging technologies blur the private and professional lives of many people online. "I honestly have to say that people have too much faith in the Internet," Gloria Gadsden said about her dilemma. "I think the Internet can be

---

6. *Bytes and Pieces*, December 9, 2009. www.aclunc.org/issues/technology/blog/ facebook_privacy_in_transition_-_but_where_is_it_heading.shtml.
7. Facebook blog, February 17, 2010. http://blog.facebook.com/blog.php?post=31105 6167130.

as dangerous as it is wonderful."[8] The privacy of Americans—as consumers, workers, students, travelers, patients, and citizens—are debated in *Opposing Viewpoints: Privacy* in the following chapters: Do Counterterrorism Measures Infringe on Privacy Rights? Do Technological Developments Threaten Privacy? Is Medical Privacy Adequately Protected? and How Should Privacy Be Protected? The friction of opinions and positions speak of the legal, constitutional, and ethical quandaries of this civil right.

8. *USA Today*, March 2, 2010. www.usatoday.com/news/education/2010-03-02-facebook-professors_N.htm.

Chapter 1

Do Counterterrorism Measures Infringe on Privacy Rights?

Chapter Preface

On Christmas Day in 2009, a passenger attempted to explode Northwest Airlines Flight 253 while it descended into Detroit's Metro Airport from the Netherlands. Umar Abdulmutallab, a twenty-three-year-old Nigerian, allegedly lit a bomb hidden in his underwear with a syringe filled with acid, igniting but failing to detonate it. Passenger Jasper Schuringa, a thirty-two-year-old Dutch filmmaker, saw Abdulmutallab on fire with a burning device between his legs. Schuringa seized it, put it out with his bare hands, and subdued the would-be bomber in the aisle. All 289 passengers and 11 crewmembers landed safely, with only Abdulmatallab, Schuringa, and another passenger suffering injuries and the plane sustaining minor damage. As of July 2010, Abdulmatallab was in custody in Michigan and faced six criminal counts, including attempting to use a weapon of mass destruction.

A university student from one of Africa's wealthiest families, Abdulmatallab told authorities that he was carrying out instructions from terrorist group al Qaeda. Alhaji Umaru Mutallab, the terror suspect's father, said he was surprised that his son was permitted to fly to the United States and had reported his "extreme religious views" to Central Intelligence Agency (CIA) officials at the U.S. Embassy in Nigeria on November 19, 2009. As a result Abdulmatallab's name was added to a roster of individuals with possible associations, but not placed on the no-fly list. "This individual should not have been missed," said Susan Collins, a senator from Maine and ranking minority member of the Homeland Security and Governmental Affairs Committee. "Clearly, there should have been a red flag next to his name."[1]

Because the USA Patriot Act allows law enforcement at airport security checkpoints to search a passenger and his or

1. *New York Times*, December 28, 2009. www.nytimes.com/2009/12/28/us/28terror.html.

her personal items without a mandate, critics were outraged at the attempted attack. "When we travel we give up not only our time but also our privacy, having all of our belongings examined and even being legally required to undergo a random body search," argues *City on a Hill Press*, the student newspaper of the University of California, Santa Cruz. "The recent attempted terrorist attack is evidence that despite the billions of dollars that have been spent on intelligence programs and watch lists since 2001, the government has not lived up to its promises of increased security."[2]

Nonetheless, supporters of the Patriot Act allege that it effectively deters terrorism. On December 27, 2009, White House press secretary Robert Gibbs appeared on *Face the Nation* and stated that "in many ways, this system has worked. We just have to continue to keep refining it and stay ahead of what terrorists are trying to do." Responding to the assertion that Mutallab's father had approached the CIA, Gibbs said, "There was not enough information to bring him more forward to either the selectee or the no-fly database list."[3] In the following chapter, the authors debate whether the USA Patriot Act and other measures against domestic terrorism protect Americans or are ineffective and invade their privacy.

2. *City on a Hill Press*, January 7, 2010. www.cityonahillpress.com/2010/01/07/still-no-security-in-the-skies/.
3. www.realclearpolitics.com/articles/2009/12/27/robert_gibbs_reps_king_clyburn_on_face_the_nation_99697.html.

| *"The Patriot Act itself was a grab bag of commonsense modifications, drafted . . . to update our surveillance laws for a world of e-mail, cell phones, and texting."*

Patriot Act Surveillance Powers Protect Americans

John Yoo

In the following viewpoint, John Yoo contends that the USA Patriot Act works to deter acts of terrorism with minimal infringements on privacy rights. Yoo argues that abuses are rare and exaggerated in the media by opponents of the Act and politicians. And he states that political activities and expression have not been suppressed by the law. In fact, Yoo concludes, civil liberties are increased during peacetime and national security policies have evolved. Yoo is a visiting fellow at the American Enterprise Institute, a nonprofit, nonpartisan think tank.

As you read, consider the following questions:

1. According to the author, critics have created what impression of the Patriot Act?

John Yoo, "Security vs. Freedom: A Balance Kept," *Philadelphia Inquirer*, March 15, 2009. Copyright © 2010 by Philadelphia Inquirer. All rights reserved. Reproduced by permission.

2. How does Yoo describe the "new enemy" within the United States?

3. What examples does the author provide to support his assertion that the Patriot Act has not infringed on civil liberties?

R ecently, the Justice Department released legal memoranda, written in the aftermath of September 11, 2001 that outlined contingency planning for further attacks on the United States. Civil libertarians are deliberately creating the misimpression that this, along with the Patriot Act and electronic surveillance of terrorist targets, was the product of a Republican administration chafing at the bit to take away civil liberties.

Nothing could be further from the truth. Many lawyers throughout the government, of which I was one, worked on what once had been unthinkable—Mumbai [India]-style terrorist attacks against civilians on U.S. soil—under intense time pressures. Agree or not with its policies, the [George W.] Bush administration succeeded in preventing another al-Qaeda attack, with any reduction in civil liberties far less than previous U.S. wars.

Certainly, history has to make anyone wary of increased police powers. Yet it is also true that U.S. law and politics have evolved since the days of the Alien and Sedition Acts [1798] or the Palmer raids [1919–1921]. Abuses that occur today are more likely to be isolated and individual acts, mistakes, rather than wholesale deprivations of civil liberties. Our career government officials are keenly respectful of law and the Bill of Rights—notwithstanding the bad-cop stereotypes and exaggerated partisanship that stirs media excitement.

An Orwellian State?

Critics would have us believe that the government is dragging us into an Orwellian security state [referring to novelist

George Orwell's portrayal of civil injustices]. Legal academics, for example, have warned that the Patriot Act endangers civil liberties. What most of this criticism amounts to is the valid point that any increase in national security might potentially infringe on civil liberties.

The rhetoric intensified with the 2004 presidential campaign. Former Vice President Al Gore, calling for the Patriot Act's repeal, accused the [George W.] Bush administration of using "fear as a political tool to consolidate its power and to escape any accountability for its use." Then-candidate Howard Dean denounced it as "morally wrong." The American Civil Liberties Union persuaded several city councils to pass symbolic resolutions refusing to obey the act and some librarians to file lawsuits against its expanded surveillance powers.

Yet, the Patriot Act itself was a grab bag of commonsense modifications, drafted primarily by career civil servants in the law enforcement and intelligence communities, to update our surveillance laws for a world of e-mail, cell phones, and texting.

It would be a grave mistake to believe that the Patriot Act and like measures represent a great leap forward in our abilities to stop terrorist attacks. We face a new enemy within our borders that is resourceful, adaptable, determined, dangerous, and highly skilled at escaping detection. Its attacks are the products of technologies, ideologies, and global dynamics entirely unknown to the world that existed after World War II and the Cold War.

Just as government can go too far in favor of security, it can also go too far in the other direction. Fear of sharing information between government agencies, for example, undoubtedly contributed to the Sept. 11 attacks.

After President Richard M. Nixon's use of the CIA [Central Intelligence Agency] and National Security Agency [NSA] to harass his political enemies, Congress passed a law that was read to block almost all sharing of information between the

CIA and the NSA, on the one hand, and the FBI [Federal Bureau of Investigation] on the other.

This "wall" prevented our intelligence and law enforcement agencies from sharing information on terrorism before 9/11. The CIA even had the identities of two of the hijackers who were in the United States, but could not share its find with the FBI. Insufficient attention to security prevented the government from "connecting the dots" to al-Qaeda, and perhaps stopping the 9/11 attacks.

The threat of an out-of-control executive seeking to harry its political enemies is not what looms before us. Legitimate political activities and exercises in speech by U.S. citizens have not been suppressed. There is no lack of lawyers to defend terrorism cases for free. In the last two elections, voters have turned out the party in power from Congress and the presidency.

The Absolutist Position

Civil libertarians often take the absolutist position that any wartime reduction of civil liberties will permanently diminish them in peacetime. Others say that panic will always lead government to go too far, or that majorities will always abuse power to oppress minorities.

U.S. history does not bear this out. Civil liberties throughout our history have expanded in peacetime and contracted during emergencies. During the Civil War, the two world wars, and the Cold War, Congress and the president restricted civil liberties, and courts deferred; during peacetime, civil liberties expanded.

Wars in the past led presidents to go far beyond anything the Bush administration did with regard to civil liberties. During the Civil War, President Abraham Lincoln suspended habeas corpus [the protection from unlawful detention] on his own authority, detained up to 14,000 U.S. civilians, and insti-

The Same Effective Tools

The Patriot Act has enhanced the fight against terrorists in four key areas:

1. it has removed obstacles to investigating terrorism

2. it has strengthened the criminal laws against terrorism

3. it has enhanced the federal government's capacity to share intelligence

4. it has updated the law to keep pace with tremendous advances in technology. . . .

The Patriot Act gives investigators the ability to fight terror, using many of the same court-approved tools that have been used successfully for many years in drug, fraud, and organized crime cases. Do the critics . . . believe that law enforcement should not use these same tools to protect Americans from terrorists?

Thomas Anderson,
Burlington (VT) Free Press, August 3, 2004.

tuted military courts for their trial. FDR [President Franklin D. Roosevelt] interned 100,000 loyal Japanese Americans during World War II.

Wars can lead to social and economic upheavals that end in expansions of individual freedom. The Union liberated the slaves and expanded individual rights against the states during Reconstruction. Civil liberties surged in the decades after World War II.

War no doubt expands executive power. But if we think executive power is an unalloyed negative, then we should reduce the administrative state, too. Oppression of minorities for self-interested gain can occur in wartime and out. Slavery and Jim Crow [segregation laws] were the products of peace, not war.

So far, nothing like the infringements on civil liberties of past wars has occurred. Only three U.S. citizens have been detained by the military. Former President George W. Bush established military courts to try terrorists for war crimes, but no citizens were included. America has been solicitous of the Arab-American community, repeatedly stating that the war is not against Arabs or Muslims, opposing racial profiling at airport searches, and prosecuting racially motivated assaults on Arab Americans.

Critics have exaggerated the threat to civil liberties today. This is not to say that constraints on the executive branch should not occur. The government's powers have been expanded. Privacy has been slightly reduced, though much more by the sheer march of communications technology than by the government.

The question is not whether some imaginary perfect world of civil liberties has been destroyed, because we do not live in that world. What we should ask of the Bush administration and its successor is whether they struck the right balance between security policies and civil liberties.

"To what degree can invasions of privacy be justified by the need to investigate and prevent acts of terrorism?"

Patriot Act Surveillance Powers Violate Privacy

Los Angeles Times

In the following viewpoint, the Los Angeles Times *claims that some provisions of the USA Patriot Act overstep privacy rights. Court orders for the seizure of business records and other documents have been restricted, the* Times *claims, but fall short of a satisfactory privacy standard. Furthermore, the author alleges that the extension of national security letters, which allows the Federal Bureau of Investigation (FBI) to search records without warrants, infringes on citizens' right to privacy. Established in 1881, the* Los Angeles Times *is California's largest daily newspaper.*

As you read, consider the following questions:

1. What does the Patriot Act symbolize, in the view of the *Los Angeles Times*?

2. What is the *Los Angeles Times*'s position on the extension of the lone wolf provision?

Los Angeles Times, "Privacy and the Patriot Act," October 25, 2009. Copyright © 2009 Los Angeles Times. Reproduced by permission.

3. According to the newspaper, why are the criteria for issuing national security letters still too vague?

Along with the Guantanamo Bay detention facility and the
[George W.] Bush administration's illegal eavesdropping
on U.S. citizens, the USA Patriot Act came to symbolize the
excesses of the post-9/11 war on terrorism. Now, as it weighs
the extension of three expiring provisions, the Democratic-
controlled Congress has an opportunity to restore key privacy
protections that were forgotten in the aftermath of the attacks.

Earlier [in October 2009], the Senate Judiciary Committee
approved a bill to renew the provisions and sent it to the Senate floor. Unfortunately, though the bill is an improvement
over current law, it still falls short. The full Senate and House
... can do better.

The USA Patriot Act, supported by members of Congress
from both parties and signed by President George W. Bush
only 6 1/2 weeks after 9/11, is formally known as the Uniting
and Strengthening America by Providing Appropriate Tools
Required to Intercept and Obstruct Terrorism Act of 2001.
The grandiose title, like the law's hasty enactment, reflected
the national resolve to do something, anything, to prevent a
repeat of 9/11.

Some parts of the original act were relatively uncontrover-
sial, including those permitting the CIA [Central Intelligence
Agency] and the FBI [Federal Bureau of Investigation] to
share information more freely and allowing investigators to
seek warrants for "roving wiretaps" targeted at individuals
rather than telephone numbers. Others, however, unjustifiably
eroded privacy rights. Particularly troubling were rules gov-
erning the acquisition of financial and other records that allowed investigators to conduct fishing expeditions—as long as
the documents were deemed "relevant" to a search for terrorists.

In December [2009], three provisions of the Patriot Act
are set to expire: those dealing with roving wiretaps and the

© 2005 Signe Wilkinson. All rights reserved.

Signe Wilkinson, "Ok. Which was the librarian who wouldn't turn over her files?" Signe Wilkinson's editorial cartoons, December 15, 2005.

acquisition of records, and another (added in 2004) that allows surveillance of what are known as "lone wolf" terrorist suspects. All three extensions strike us as reasonable, though in one case further privacy protections are essential.

In the era of disposable cellphones, it makes sense for investigators, with a court order, to be able to listen in on a targeted suspect's calls regardless of where he is. And roving wiretaps long have been used in criminal investigations.

Loose Standards for Court Orders

More problematic is the provision allowing court orders for business records and other "tangible things"—popularly known as the "library records" provision because of fears that investigators would monitor the reading habits of citizens (even though the law doesn't mention library records specifically). The Judiciary Committee bill explicitly makes it harder to obtain library records and requires investigators to show a court that the material sought is reasonably likely to be relevant to an intelligence investigation. Under current law, by contrast, a judge is supposed to presume that the materials are relevant. Even with that refinement, "relevance to an investigation" is too loose a standard for a court order. As Senators Russell D. Feingold (D-Wis.) and Richard J. Durbin (D-Ill.) proposed, the bill should be revised to require a tighter connection to a particular foreign agent or terrorist.

Finally, the bill would extend the lone wolf provision, under which investigators can seek a warrant to spy on a suspected terrorist even if he is not affiliated with a foreign power or organized terrorist group. Critics argue that this provision—which the [Barack] Obama administration says has never been employed—is unnecessary because any suspected terrorist acting alone could be investigated under criminal laws. True, but the collection of foreign intelligence had previously been subject to rules different from those of a criminal investigation. On balance, the committee was right to extend this provision. Not every foreign terrorist is a card-carrying member of Al Qaeda [terrorist organization linked to 9/11 attacks] and thus is not always so easily spotted and monitored.

The Patriot Act's greatest threat to personal privacy lies not in any of the provisions set to expire but in the law's expansion of the use of national security letters, subpoenas that allow the FBI to obtain records without a warrant. In 2008, the FBI issued 24,744 letters involving the records of 7,225 people. Not surprisingly, there have been abuses. In 2007, after an investigation of four FBI offices, the Justice Department's inspector general found irregularities in 22% of documents related to the issuance of national security letters. [In 2008], he found that the FBI had made "significant progress" in correcting violations.

More Transparency and Accountability

Even so, the criteria for issuing the letters are too vague. At present, the government must merely certify that the information sought is relevant to an authorized investigation. The bill approved by the Judiciary Committee would increase the burden on the government slightly by requiring a written statement of specific facts demonstrating relevance. A narrower amendment by Feingold and Durbin—which would have required issuance of national security letters to be related to a suspected foreign agent or terrorist or a possible confederate—was rejected by the committee. It should be added on the Senate floor or in an eventual conference with the House.

The other problem with national security letters is that the companies or other institutions that receive them are not allowed to reveal that fact publicly, though they can appeal them in a closed hearing in federal District Court. Feingold proposed that the government certify that disclosure of the request would result in serious harm, and that the gag be lifted in a year's time unless the government presented new evidence that secrecy was necessary. The final version of the Patriot Act extension legislation should include those safeguards.

The committee also approved new limits on "sneak and peek" searches of a property conducted in the absence of the owner or resident. Currently, the targets of such searches must be informed within 30 days after the search; the committee reduced that to seven days.

It's easy amid this welter of technical provisions to lose sight of the overarching question: To what degree can invasions of privacy be justified by the need to investigate and prevent acts of terrorism? In the aftermath of 9/11, both Congress and the executive branch needlessly cut legal corners. It's time to make amends.

> *"Searching a computer without suspicion* unnecessarily *exposes a plethora of private information that would not otherwise be available to law enforcement authorities."*

Laptop Searches of Travelers Violate Privacy

Ira Winkler

In the following viewpoint, Ira Winkler opposes suspicionless and random laptop searches for travelers on several grounds. First, he maintains that searching electronics would violate privacy: Laptops and handheld devices contain extensive records, health data, and other sensitive information. Second, Winkler alleges that unlike physical searches, electronic searches are time-consuming and would divert officers and agents from performing other duties and safeguards. Ultimately, the Homeland Security's Privacy Office does not, the author insists, grasp the complexities of data confiscation or encryption. Winkler is the president of Internet Security Advisors Group and the author of Spies Among Us.

Ira Winkler, "Opinion: Suspicionless Laptop Searches Are Wrong for Many Reasons," *Computerworld*, September 2, 2009. Copyright © 2010 Computerworld. Reproduced by permission.

As you read, consider the following questions:

1. As stated by Winkler, how is carrying physical contraband different from carrying a laptop?

2. How does Winkler back his claim that the Privacy Office does not fully understand data encryption?

3. What is the author's advice for travelers who are subjected to a laptop search?

I have generally supported the government's border search policies. But I am horrified by the recent DHS [Department of Homeland Security] Privacy Office's approval of searches of electronic devices without suspicion. It is wrong for many reasons; from the constitutional to the logistical.

Government does have the right to conduct searches when there is even a slight reason for suspicion. I wouldn't want to impede the intuition of well-seasoned U.S. Immigration and Customs Enforcement [ICE] officers. They are on the front lines, and it is reasonable to give them some latitude. But that doesn't extend to pulling someone out just because they feel like it.

Constitutionally, this policy has been examined by others more knowledgeable than me. Suffice to say that it is horrifying that a U.S. citizen on U.S. soil could be subject to illegal search and seizure on the basis of . . . nothing—no evidence, and not even a shred of suspicion.

Beyond that, though, there is the dubious opinion of the Department of Homeland Security's Privacy Office that searching electronic devices is no different than searching a briefcase or backpack. That is one of the most clueless statements to come out of the DHS. It is a simple matter to show that a person caught with physical contraband had the intent to carry that property. It's a lot harder to argue that all the data on a person's computer is there by the volition of that person. And searching a laptop computer is a much greater violation of one's privacy than searching a suitcase. Laptops often contain data that would never be physically carried by a traveler, such as bank records, health data and information about relatives and friends. And a corporate device could contain sensitive information, company secrets, data that the company is bound by law to protect. Do we really want ICE officers making copies of such information? If there was a legitimate suspicion to justify the search, I wouldn't object to any of that information being exposed to the searchers. But searching a computer without suspicion *unnecessarily* exposes a plethora of private information that would not otherwise be available to law enforcement authorities. Bureaucrats should always place themselves in the shoes of those they are regulating before writing policies. I would have liked to have seen the staff of the Privacy Office make their personal laptops available to the public before they made this ruling.

Targeting Computer-Related Crimes

And here is a question to ponder: What type of crimes are you looking for when you conduct a suspicionless search? The interest of ICE officers presumably is to find information that protects the country from outside harm and to make sure that people properly declare information upon entering the country. But computer-related crimes are not abetted by being overseas. If a known criminal is entering the country with electronic devices in tow, I'd say go ahead and search the devices. In the absence of any suspicion at all, I'd expect restraint.

Finally, consider the logistics of laptop data searches. They take exponentially more time and training to perform than physical searches. An ICE officer who lacks the proper training for such searches is not going to find anything that an actual criminal wants to hide on his computer. Such a search is certain to be a waste of time. If the agency does come up with properly trained officers to do these searches, suspicionless searches will still be a waste of time—just a lot more time. Pulling data off of a laptop takes a lot of time, even if the data are just being copied. And then there is the issue of losing access to your own data for an extended period of time, which I'll discuss below.

Suspicionless searches will also open the door to training searches. I have been subjected to random physical searches at airports many times because a new officer was in training. Those searches took only a minute or so and were not a major inconvenience. But a training search of a computer will be a time-consuming inconvenience that unnecessarily exposes data to untrained people.

More critical than wasting travelers' time, though, is wasting the time of agents. After the 9/11 [2001 terrorist] attacks, airports implemented random searches. Among those searched back then were toddlers and former Vice President Al Gore. While Gore might have been upset with the manner in which he lost the 2000 presidential election, I don't think anyone seriously thought he could be a danger to a commercial airline. Other than the toddlers, I doubt that there was anyone in line who was a less imminent danger than Gore. But random searches were the order of the day, and officers were diverted from doing things that might have actually safeguarded the transportation system. Now, with suspicionless searches of electronic devices, agents will be diverted once again from doing searches that are motivated by legitimate cause. This is a problem because our resources are not limitless. We must use our limited resources as best we can, and that means at least limiting searches to those with suspicion.

The Consequences of Laptop Confiscation

So, let's say that your computer has been singled out for a search. What happens with the data? It is likely that the DHS will make copies of it. But the agents might decide to confiscate the computer, and they don't have to have a reason for

Going Too Far

I guarantee you this: neither the drafters of the Fourth Amendment [which protects from unwarranted search and seizure], nor the Supreme Court when it crafted the "border search exception," ever dreamed that tens of thousands of Americans would cross the border every day, carrying with them the equivalent of a full library of their most personal information. Ideally, Fourth Amendment jurisprudence would evolve to protect Americans' privacy in this once unfathomable situation. But if the courts can't offer that protection, then that responsibility falls to Congress. Customs agents must have the ability to conduct even highly intrusive searches when there is reason to suspect criminal or terrorist activity, but suspicionless searches of Americans' laptops and similar devices go too far.

Russ Feingold,
Senate Judiciary Committee,
June 25, 2008.

doing so. They could even do it just for training purposes. What then? You should worry about that, because the DHS has a history of compromised data, meaning it has botched the handling of its own data, held on machines it was presumably familiar with. Should we expect the DHS, then, to handle your confiscated data any better?

The DHS would like to calm your fears with the promise that it will encrypt data, "where needed." This is an example of how clueless the DHS Privacy Office is. The statement presumes there will be instances when encryption is not needed. But given that the ICE is collecting data without suspicion, then by definition the ICE does not know what data these devices hold. Shouldn't, then, the default setting be to encrypt and ask questions later?

But if the DHS did decide that your data should be encrypted, should you take any comfort in that? I wouldn't. If your laptop is confiscated, the DHS would have to encrypt the entire device, where no encryption is likely to exist. Encrypting a laptop can be very complicated and, if not properly done, can destroy all the data. But assuming the DHS does manage to do the encryption properly, will you ever regain access to all your data? I have my doubts there as well. It just amazes me that the Privacy Office does not seem to understand all the issues that accompany data encryption.

And confiscation is another area where the Privacy Office's contention that this new policy is no different from what applies to backpacks is laughably suspect. If a backpack is confiscated, it can be easily and inexpensively replaced, and any information it contained is likely minimal. But a laptop is a major expense, not easily replaced. We all know we should back up our data, but most of us still don't do it as often as we should. And even those of us who are fanatical about backups tend to slack off when we're traveling. People whose devices are confiscated will therefore be denied access to their own data and could suffer drastic consequences. I'm talking about small businesses that are forced to close because they couldn't bear the expense of replacing a laptop and all its software licenses, or students who fail classes because they don't have access to their notes. Grim consequences for something done on the whim of an ICE officer.

How Not to Handle All This

This is a bad policy, but don't think the answer to it is to try to hide your data. Some people have advocated encrypting drives and then refusing to provide the password to customs officials. This is terrible advice that will surely lead to confiscation and arrest. Such unusual precautions to prevent the examination of your information will automatically justify suspicion. You can claim that you are attempting to protect your civil liberties, and good luck with that. The officers confronting you are not going to congratulate you on your knowledge of the Constitution. They are going to see you as someone who is employing the same tactics as criminals. In their eyes, you will look suspicious. That is their job.

The majority of ICE officers are well-meaning and do not want to inconvenience anyone unnecessarily. They take their jobs to heart and see their work as necessary to stopping clear and present threats to the country. I respect their intentions. That does not mean that I want them to have the ability to do whatever they want.

And as bad as all this sounds, remember that when you, a U.S. citizen, enter a foreign country, you have no rights at all.

> "To treat digital media at the interna-
> tional border differently . . . would pro-
> vide a great advantage to terrorists and
> others who seek to do us harm."

Laptop Searches of Travelers Do Not Violate Privacy

Jayson P. Ahern

*In the following viewpoint, Jayson P. Ahern writes that suspi-
cionless searches of travelers' laptops and electronic devices respect privacy and protect Americans. According to the author,
these procedures comply with constitutional rights and other
laws at U.S. borders and have been consistently upheld by the
courts. In fact, Ahern proposes that laptop searches hinder terrorists and their allies as well as crack down on child pornography and piracy. While searching without suspicion is permitted,
he maintains that agents and officers observe telltale facts, behaviors, and circumstances on an individual basis. Ahern is the
acting commissioner of U.S. Customs and Border Protection.*

Jayson P. Ahern, "Laptop Searches and Other Violations of Privacy Faced by Americans
Returning from Overseas Travel," U.S. Customs and Border Protection. www.cbp.gov,
June 25, 2008.

As you read, consider the following questions:

1. What examples does the author provide to support his argument that the courts favor suspicionless searches of electronic devices?

2. How are travelers connected to countries associated with terrorism treated at U.S. borders, as stated by Ahern?

3. Why was Michael Arnold subjected to an electronics search at an airport, according to the author?

I am pleased to submit this testimony . . . to discuss U.S. Customs and Border Protection (CBP) policies and practices with regard to searching the contents of laptops and other digital devices at our nation's ports of entry. My testimony today will provide you with specific information that the subcommittee has requested on how CBP inspects these items.

At the outset, I want to emphasize that CBP disagrees with the premise contained in this hearing's title [Laptop Searches and other Violations of Privacy Faced by Americans Returning from Overseas Travel]: CBP's efforts do not infringe on Americans' privacy. It is important to keep in mind that CBP is responsible for enforcing over 600 laws at the border, including those that relate to narcotics, intellectual property, child pornography and other contraband, and terrorism. CBP's ability to examine what is coming into the country is crucial to its ability to enforce U.S. law and keep the country safe from terrorism. This notion is not novel. As the U.S. Supreme Court has stated, "since the beginning of our Government," the Executive Branch has enjoyed "plenary authority to conduct routine searches and seizures at the border, without probable cause or a warrant, in order to regulate the collection of duties and to prevent the introduction of contraband into this country."

Searches of Digital Devices Constitutional

More recently, federal courts throughout the country have recognized that CBP's efforts at the border with respect to digital devices—like our efforts with respect to vehicles, suitcases, backpacks, containers of hard-copy documents, and other conveyances—are consistent with long-standing constitutional authority at the U.S. border and other laws. This past April [2008], in *United States v. Arnold*, the U.S. Court of Appeals for the Ninth Circuit upheld the suspicionless search of an international traveler's laptop computer that uncovered child pornography, stating that "[c]ourts have long held that searches of closed containers and their contents can be conducted at the border." Likewise, in 2006 a U.S. citizen was convicted following the discovery of child pornography on his laptop during a border search. The Ninth Circuit refused to vacate the conviction. And a similar conclusion was reached by the U.S. Court of Appeals for the Fourth Circuit in *United States v. Ickes*, which also involved a conviction for possession of child pornography.

In addition to several successes in arresting individuals possessing child pornography, CBP border searches also have been helpful in limiting the movement of terrorists, individuals who support their activities and threats to national security. During border searches of laptops CBP officers have found violent jihadist material, information about cyanide and nuclear material, video clips of Improvised Explosive Devices (IEDs) being exploded, pictures of various high-level Al-Qaida [the terrorist organization linked to the attacks of September 11, 2001,] officials and other material associated with people seeking to do harm to U.S. and its citizens. These materials have led to the refusal [of] admission and the removal of these dangerous people from the United States.

Another example of how a border search led to disruption of a national security threat is the case of Xuedong Sheldon Meng. In November 2004, ICE [Immigration and Customs

Enforcement] agents learned that Meng, a Canadian national, allegedly stole proprietary software programs from a U.S. company and attempted to sell the software to the People's Republic of China (PRC). Two of the software programs are both controlled items for export under the AECA [Arms Export Control Act] and the International Traffic in Arms Regulations (ITAR). On December 6, 2004, Meng traveled from China to Orlando, Florida, to attend a defense conference. ICE agents coordinated with CBP to conduct a border search of Meng and his belongings when he entered the United States at Minneapolis, Minnesota. During the search, CBP officers identified a laptop computer and portable hard drive belonging to Meng. A preliminary search of the laptop revealed that it contained software belonging to the American company which is a controlled item for export under ITAR.

On June 18, 2008, Meng, was sentenced in the Northern District of California to two years incarceration for violations of 18 USC 1831, the Economic Espionage Act; and 22 USC 2778, the Arms Export Control Act. Meng also received a $10,000 fine and 3 years probation. Additionally, this is the first ICE case involving a conviction under 18 USC 1831. This is also the first conviction and sentencing for violations of 22 USC 2778 involving computer software. This joint ICE and FBI [Federal Bureau of Investigation] investigation was made possible by information gained by the initial CBP border search of his laptop and portable hard drive.

Twin Goals Are at Stake

CBP and Immigration and Customs Enforcement (ICE) continue to carry out border searches within their legal authorities and have been able to arrest criminals and limit the entrance of dangerous people to the U.S. as a result. To treat digital media at the international border differently than CBP has treated documents and other conveyances historically would provide a great advantage to terrorists and others who seek to do us harm. As the U.S. Court of Appeals for the Sec-

A Tiny Percentage

Of the approximately 400 million travelers who entered the country last year [2007], only a tiny percentage were referred to secondary baggage inspection for a more thorough examination. Of those, only a fraction had electronic devices that may have been checked.

Michael Chertoff, USA Today, July 16, 2008.

ond Circuit stated in the case *United States v. Irving,* which upheld the border search of luggage and a subsequent search of a camera and computer diskettes, treating the computer diskettes differently than other closed containers "would allow individuals to render graphic contraband, such as child pornography, largely immune to border search simply by scanning images onto a computer disk before arriving at the border." The same could be said for terrorist communications. Indeed, the Fourth Circuit in *United States v. Ickes* rejected an argument that additional protections should apply to certain material contained on computers, stating that this logic "would create a sanctuary at the border" for all such material, "even for terrorist plans."

As America's frontline border agency, CBP employs highly trained and professional personnel, resources, expertise, and law enforcement authorities to meet our twin goals of improving security and facilitating the flow of legitimate trade and travel. CBP is responsible for preventing terrorists and terrorist weapons from entering the United States, for apprehending individuals attempting to enter the United States illegally, and stemming the flow of illegal drugs and other contraband. We also are protecting our agricultural and economic interests from harmful pests and diseases and safeguarding American businesses from theft of their intellectual property.

Finally, we are regulating and facilitating international trade, collecting import duties, and enforcing United States trade laws.

One goal of the CBP inspection process is to establish that a person attempting to enter the United States does not pose a threat to the safety and welfare of our nation. Our ability to search information contained in documents and electronic devices, including laptops, is just one enforcement tool aimed at defending against these threats. As you know, all persons, baggage, and other merchandise arriving in or departing from the United States are subject to inspection and search by CBP officers. As part of the inspection process, officers verify the identity of persons, determine the admissibility of aliens, and look for possible terrorists, terrorist weapons, controlled substances, and a wide variety of other prohibited and restricted items. Every person seeking to enter the United States must be examined by a CBP officer at a designated port of entry. This may include checking names and conveyances in law enforcement databases; examining entry and identity documents; examining belongings and conveyances; collecting biometric information where applicable; and questioning the traveler.

Aliens have the burden of establishing that they are admissible to the U.S., or are entitled to the immigration status they seek. U.S. citizens also have to establish their citizenship to the satisfaction of the officer and may be subject to further inspection if they are the subject of a lookout record, if there are indicators of possible violations (such as the possible possession of prohibited items, narcotics, or other contraband), or if they have been selected for random compliance examination.

Constitutional and Statutory Safeguards

At the Senate Judiciary Committee's hearing on the oversight of the Department of Homeland Security (DHS), held on April 2, 2008, a question was asked about the inspection of individuals with connections to countries associated with significant terrorist activity. At that hearing, Secretary [Michael] Chertoff stated that, "U.S. citizens are not treated differently based upon their ethnic background, but their individualized behavior could be a basis for singling them out, or if they matched a physical description it could be a basis for singling them out." One of the primary objectives of the CBP inspection process is to establish that a person is lawfully entering the United States, and does not pose a threat to the safety and welfare of our nation. Thus, an individual's frequent travel to countries associated with significant terrorist activity, narcotics smuggling, or sexual exploitation of minors, may give our officers reason to question that person's reasons for travel. When officers are satisfied that the person has valid reasons for the frequent travel, and there are no other areas of concern or potential violations, the person may be cleared to enter the United States. There are no special rules for personal belongings or documents. However, CBP does enforce numerous laws concerning material in paper or electronic form, both of which are treated the same conceptually and constitutionally. For example, U.S. laws prohibit the importation of child pornography, that constitutes pirated intellectual property, or that contains any threat to take the life of or inflict bodily harm upon any person.

In regards to the privacy of these searches, CBP officers conduct their work in a manner designed to adhere to all constitutional and statutory requirements, including those that are applicable to privileged, personal, and business confidential information. The Trade Secrets Act prohibits federal employees from disclosing, without lawful authority, business confidential information to which they obtain access as part of their official duties. Moreover, CBP has strict policies and procedures that implement constitutional and statutory safeguards through internal policies that compel regular review and purging of information that is no longer relevant. CBP will protect information that may be discovered during the examination process, as well as private information of a personal nature that is not in violation of any law.

One example of an instance where CBP determined it necessary to conduct a search of a laptop computer and other electronic equipment occurred on July 17, 2005, when a Michael Arnold arrived at Los Angeles International Airport on a flight from Manila, Philippines. Mr. Arnold was selected for a secondary examination, and exhibited nervous behavior when questioned about the purpose of travel to Manila. After failing to provide consistent answers about the individual's occupation and purpose of travel, a declaration was obtained and the individual's luggage was inspected. Upon the inspection of the laptop and CDs found in the individual's luggage, officers found images of adults molesting children. U.S. Immigration and Customs Enforcement (ICE) then conducted an interview of the individual and searched the contents of the individual's laptop, CDs, and memory stick. These items were detained, and turned over to ICE for investigation. During his subsequent prosecution, the district court suppressed the evidence on the ground that the search violated the Constitution. The government appealed, and the lower court's decision was overturned by the Ninth Circuit, which held that "reasonable suspicion is not needed for customs officials to search a laptop or other personal electronic storage devices at the border." As the U.S. Supreme Court noted in the [*United States v.*] *Flores-Montano* decision in 2004, the Government's interest in preventing the entry of unwanted persons and effects—and the corresponding search authority of the sovereign—is at its zenith at the international border.

Resources Are Limited

It is important to understand that CBP typically encounters well over a million travelers every day and is responsible for enforcing over 600 federal laws at the border. CBP does not have the resources to conduct searches on every laptop or cell phone that pass through our ports of entry, nor is there a need to do so. When we do conduct a search, it is often premised on facts, circumstances, and inferences which give rise to individualized suspicion, even though the courts have repeatedly confirmed that such individualized suspicion is not required under the law.

CBP's frontline officers and agents will continue to protect America from terrorist threats and accomplish our traditional enforcement missions in immigration, customs, and agriculture, while balancing the need to facilitate legitimate trade and travel. As I mentioned, the initiatives discussed today are only a portion of CBP's efforts to secure our homeland, and we will continue to provide our men and women on the frontlines with the necessary tools to help them gain effective control of our Nation's borders.

| "The reality is that today, the current licensing and personal identification systems are regularly exploited."

A National Identity Card Would Preserve Privacy

Sandra Kay Miller

In the following viewpoint, Sandra Kay Miller asserts that a unified identification system would thwart terrorism, fraud, and identity theft. The author claims that the REAL ID Act of 2005 calls for standardized "smart card" technology for driver's licenses and ID cards, which makes counterfeiting and tampering much more difficult. Despite fears and speculations, REAL ID is neither intended to serve as a national identification card nor create a federal database of personal information, Miller says. Miller is a writer based in Newburg, Pennsylvania.

As you read, consider the following questions:

1. According to Brian Zimmer, what types of identification were the September 11 terrorists able to obtain?

2. How did opponents react to REAL ID, as told by Miller?

Sandra Kay Miller, "REAL ID Backlash," *Access Control & Security Systems Integration*, vol. 51, December 2, 2008. Copyright © 2008 Penton Business Media, Inc. Reproduced by permission.

3. How does Miller say states will pay for REAL ID implementation?

For private companies as well as the government and education sectors, using smart cards as a means for identification and authentication has been routine since the early 1990s. IMS Research Group predicts that by 2010, more than six billion smart cards will be deployed globally and smart cards will become the most commonly used secure method for identification throughout the world.

After the September 11 [2001] terrorist attacks and the formation of the Department of Homeland Security (DHS), the government set out to make changes that could help thwart future attacks. One of the vulnerabilities identified was the lack of a unified identification system within the country.

Out of this realization, the REAL ID Act of 2005 was passed in an effort to make state-issued driver's licenses and ID cards more difficult for illegal immigrants and terrorists to obtain. Brian Zimmer is president of the Coalition for a Secure Driver's License, a non-partisan, not-for-profit, grassroots organization whose mission is to raise public awareness about the critical need for secure driver's licenses. He says the 9/11 terrorists held more than 30 valid driver's licenses and ID cards issued by five different states, thus making them appear legitimate.

To reduce such circumvention, states would be required to authenticate original identification documents, such as Social Security cards and birth certificates, through their issuing agency. Additionally, states would be required to maintain an electronic database that could be accessed by other states to verify that duplicate licenses have not been issued by multiple states. The REAL ID laws also establish standardized security features for both the issuance and the physical card itself to further prevent counterfeiting and tampering.

Americans born after December 1, 1964 should begin receiving driver's licenses meeting the REAL ID criteria within the next six years. Older drivers would have until 2018 to comply.

Sour Reactions

When the final ruling for the REAL ID Act of 2005 was issued in January 2008, public privacy organizations, watchdog groups and many individual states reacted sourly. Citing violations of constitutional rights and cost issues, REAL ID began building up to a showdown between the federal government and individual states' rights.

American Civil Liberties Union spokesman Jay Stanley warned citizens of the impending "red tape" and referred to REAL ID as the federalization of state-issued identification. Similarly, Jim Harper, director of information policy studies at the Cato Institute, told a Senate Committee, "Having a national ID would promote a surveillance society that we should all dread."

"Smart cards for driver's licenses are a relatively new idea, and what's going to be put on the card hasn't been well articulated. The public is unsure of how they are protected and unconvinced of the value it will bring to their daily lives. If they saw a little more of the value and knew about how secure the cards are, it will lead to increasing acceptance of the use of smart cards," says Rob Brandewie, senior vice president of ActivIdentity Inc., Fremont, California, provider of digital identity assurance systems for the enterprise, government, healthcare and financial services markets.

Randy Vanderhoof, executive director of the Smart Card Alliance, a non-profit, multi-industry association working to promote the understanding, adoption, use and widespread application of smart card technology, believes the backlash is coming from people who don't want to change anything about driver's licenses that's going to cost them money. "Any pro-

Heading Off Abuse

Critics of a national ID . . . worry about police challenging members of the public, especially in minority neighborhoods, to show their national ID. But similar harassment is already possible under the current system. Further abuses can be headed off by stipulating in the law that no one would be required to present a national ID except in very specific circumstances.

Boston Globe, *"Why Not a National ID?"*
January 20, 2008.

posal that includes putting more cost and money into driver's licenses was met with opposition by those who felt that it was an unfunded mandate by the federal government and that states shouldn't be required to fund these projects out of their own pocket if the federal government wants to increase or improve the security of the nation," Vanderhoof explains.

The estimated national cost for implementing REAL ID is $4 billion. States will be able to use up to 20 percent of a state's Homeland security grant program funds for REAL ID compliance projects. Additionally, Congress will have the authority to appropriate additional funds to aid states enacting REAL ID. DHS Secretary Michael Chertoff has also promised that his agency will provide more than $360 million to help states implement REAL ID. By Chertoff's estimate, the extra $8 per license will greatly aid law enforcement in their fight against forged documents and identity theft.

Additional Costs but Also Benefits

Brandewie believes that the public would be willing to help foot the bill if it reduced the chances of falling victim to identity theft and fraud, one of the fastest growing crimes in the country. Despite the additional costs, he sees smart card technology as a valid and affordable solution. "There's no way around it, it is more expensive. Driver's licenses now typically cost less than a dollar, but good smart cards aren't going to hit that price point yet. Although, they may as volume increases. I think the price has come down on very capable smart cards to the point where they've become affordable," says Brandewie, who also points out that the increased costs are spread over the life of the license.

In an effort to get the ball rolling, the federal government set a compliance date of May 11, 2008. States must agree to comply with and begin instituting REAL ID by this deadline or be subject to consequences, which will result in their non-REAL ID compliant state-issued drivers licenses and ID cards not being accepted as valid forms of identification for boarding an airplane or entering a federal property, such as a courthouse, military base or nuclear facility.

To date, five states (Montana, South Carolina, Maine, New Hampshire and Oklahoma) have responded with a resounding "no," going so far as to enact legislation barring the state from participating in REAL ID. Sixteen states have not committed to REAL ID or requested an extension to meet the deadlines of the first phase of REAL ID. The remainder of states have agreed, although many have requested and been granted extensions and openly question whether or not they will adopt REAL ID as their deadline approaches.

Brandewie explains that states that adopt REAL ID can also use the technology to deliver state-based services to the public. He would like to see citizens using smart cards in their everyday life for access to things such as taxes, social services and, ultimately, to be able to vote from home using secure credentials. "That kind of access to government records using secure identity would be something that would be a boon to the citizens as well as for government."

Vanderhoof agrees, "Individual states don't have to limit their REAL ID-compliant driver's licenses to the federal minimum standards. They can meet the requirements of REAL ID and, at the same time, add smart card technology to further improve the security and privacy of licenses and be able to take advantage of the cost-savings derived from having a trusted secure ID credential. The credential can be used for the delivery of state government services—things like permits, administration of welfare and health assistance, car registration and first responder credentials. These could all be rolled into a state ID card that also serves as a driver's license."

More Personal Security, Not Less

Despite the fear-mongering and speculation, the REAL ID Act is not meant to create a unified national identity card. Individual states will maintain control over their individual driver's license and ID issuance. Personal information will not be warehoused in a federal database or accessed by the federal government.

The reality is that today, the current licensing and personal identification systems are regularly exploited. Vanderhoof believes that the addition of smart card technology would greatly aid in a more secure means of personal identification through state-issued licenses and identity cards.

"If smart card technology was deployed in driver's licenses, identity cards for border access and other programs like Medicaid, we'd dramatically reduce the amount of fraud that takes place with people using someone else's ID or someone altering or modifying an ID to look legitimate when it's not," he says.

| "State legislatures have rebelled against a federal edict that establishes a key component of [fascist] tyrannies: the national ID card."

A National Identity Card Would Compromise Privacy

Becky Akers

In the following viewpoint, Becky Akers argues that the 2005 REAL ID Act's successor, the Providing for Additional Security in States' Identification (PASS ID) Act of 2009, would further pry into Americans' privacy. If passed, she contends, it would force everyone to carry driver's licenses and ID cards with even more personal information. PASS ID would also increase government access to such data and situations in which citizens must present identification, Akers continues. She insists that driver's license databases are the most detailed and updated and allow the government to spy on Americans. Akers writes about the American Revolution and is a contributor to LewRockwell.com, a libertarian Web site.

Becky Akers, "'Your Papers Please!' Though REAL ID Implementation Stalled, Its Twin, PASS ID, Seems to Be Gaining Traction Because the Federal Government Is Poised to Fund the Mandate," *The New American*, vol. 25, August 31, 2009, pp. 23–27. Copyright © 2009 American Opinion Publishing Incorporated. Reproduced by permission.

As you read, consider the following questions:

1. As stated by Aker, what does the future hold with PASS ID?

2. For what reasons did governors oppose the REAL ID Act, in Aker's view?

3. How do governments control citizens through driver's licenses, in the author's opinion?

Not long ago, Americans feared and ridiculed the police states cursing too many parts of the world. We worried that they might one day conquer us despite their poverty and general misery even as we mocked their totalitarian tactics—especially their "Papers, please" mentality. Indeed, being forced to prove one's identity to a bureaucrat on demand, having to carry and produce documents with personal information for his approval—condemnation—seemed especially horrifying. One of our classic films, *Casablanca*, revolved around the deadly hassles of obtaining or forging such papers under the Nazis; episodes of *Mission Impossible* in the 1960s often featured the same detail as American agents outwitted sinister Slavic tyrants.

What tragic irony, then, that the U.S. government increasingly compels us to identify ourselves. And it's an even greater tragedy that this command no longer terrifies Americans, let alone goads them to protest.

Until now. While the president and his cronies push the country toward full-fledged fascism, state legislatures have rebelled against a federal edict that establishes a key component of such tyrannies: the national ID card.

Congress passed the REAL ID Act in 2005 as a rider on a bill handing more of our money to the military. There was no debate about either the concept of a national ID or the details of implementing it—including the astronomical costs of forcing states to convert the driver's licenses they issue into national ID cards.

That expense may explain the fiery opposition REAL ID sparked—opposition unprecedented in our lifetime. Some states forbade their bureaucracies to comply with REAL ID while others officially denounced the legislation.

Feds Are Firing Back

But the feds [federal officials] haven't surrendered. Instead, they've drafted virtually identical legislation under an alias— "Providing for Additional Security in States' Identification Act of 2009" (PASS ID)—with one difference: states keep more of the taxes they extort from us (or, as Government Technology puts it, PASS ID "reduc[es] costs by providing greater flexibility for states to meet federal requirements by eliminating fees associated with the use of existing databases"). Nevertheless, the last time a federal outrage generated this much fury, Northerners and Southerners went to war.

And an outrage it is. By whatever name, this legislation puts your driver's license on speed, ramping it up into a national ID. It dramatically increases the personal information your license contains, the number of bureaucrats who can access that data, and the circumstances when the government will not only scrutinize your ID but then decide whether you may proceed with your business—or not.

Though REAL ID wasn't and PASS ID isn't explicit about embedding a tracking chip or including biometric data such as fingerprints or retinal scans in licenses, it's likely both would occur sooner rather than later. And you'll be flashing your card so much you'll probably wear it around your neck rather than dig it out of your wallet: the feds will inspect it each time you so much as enter a location under their jurisdiction, including courthouses and airports. You'll have to show it to open a bank account as well. That custom will doubtless spread to all financial transactions, even the most picayune, as Americans become inured to the constant order, "Papers, please."

No wonder REAL ID provoked rebellion. But little of it was grassroots: except for members of organizations like the John Birch Society or Campaign for Liberty, most folks still know very little about REAL ID or PASS ID and care even less; a few actually applaud a national ID because the government claims it fights terrorism. Rather, organizations like the American Civil Liberties Union and the Electronic Frontier Foundation (which "defend[s] your rights in the digital world") led the charge. Joining them were the governors of various states in a nigh revolutionary stand-off with the feds. That's even more remarkable when we consider Washington, D.C.'s countless other anti-constitutional incursions over the last hundred years, most of which eviscerated states' sovereignty just as much as if not more than REAL ID does. Yet it was REAL ID—not affirmative action and its contempt for freedom of association, nor environmental regulations that gut property rights, nor the massacres at Waco [Texas] and Ruby Ridge [Idaho]—that finally galvanized states to defy the federal Frankenstein.

States Finally Oppose the New ID System

Why? Most of the governors opposed to REAL ID cited two reasons. They professed concern about our vanishing liberty—a concern strangely missing from their acceptance of other unconstitutional mandates, as well as their own tyrannical decrees. They also complained about its cost, which conservative estimates put somewhere around $23 billion. Yet D.C.'s dictators impose plenty of other unfunded mandates on states, and while governors complain, they don't rebel.

Still, money likely motivated their mutiny. For one thing, the National Governors Association likes PASS ID because it believes the reds have learned their lesson and will put the dollars where their bill is this time. For another, states resented spending billions on REAL ID's outlay, but that's only a tiny part of the story. Licensing drivers is a gold mine for local governments, one so lucrative that they're highly suspicious of federal interest in the process.

Indeed, the loot from licensing us, as well as the plunder from concomitant fees and fines, is so vast that no one knows the actual amount. That's partly because governments conceal their profits lest bigger, badder governments steal from them what they stole from us: municipalities often hide how much they extract in traffic tickets for fear their state will demand a bigger cut. So even in our computerized age with its sophisticated methods of accounting, no one knows how much tickets alone filch from us. The National Motorists Association estimates the amount at somewhere between $3.75 and $7.5 billion annually—and that excludes parking tickets. Now add fees for car registration, driver's licenses, license plates, title certificates, and inspections, as well as the taxes that encumber all things automotive (sales of cars, insurance, gasoline, and parking), to say nothing of parking meters and tolls. (*Newsday* reported that New York City alone collected 126 million tolls solely for crossing to and from the island of Manhattan in 2006; these ranged from a couple dollars for motorcycles to $36 or more for a truck with five axles.)

Picking our pockets on behalf of the State is one of licensing's two basic purposes, regardless of its type: professional (doctor's, realtor's, broadcasting), fishing and hunting, driver's. Linda Lewis-Pickett, president and CEO [chief executive officer] of the American Association of Motor Vehicle Administrators in 2006, frankly admitted that "each state agency has looked at DMVs [Departments of Motor Vehicles] as revenue generators—'Come in and pay taxes and give us money.'" The driver's licenses and plates those DMVs dispense also enable officials to track us to a billing address, no matter how

Vulnerable Data Dumps

DMVs [Departments of Motor Vehicles] and local governments have always been vulnerable data dumps where a stalker with a good story could potentially score an address. But DMVs were at least limited . . . ; you could move from your small town where your abuser knew a guy who knew a police officer who could demand confidential information to another state with another system. The REAL ID Act would interlink all of them, so an irresponsible or incompetent official in Arkansas could track a target in Missouri.

Kerry Howley, Reason, *February 1, 2008.*

flawed the issuing cop's judgment, regardless of how we disagree with his assessment of our speed or the length of time we paused at a stop sign.

Paternal Regulations

Licensing's other purpose is the control it grants rulers. There's a reason licenses are also known as "permits": what the government permits one day it may prohibit the next. Wielding the power to deprive a man of his livelihood or his ability to travel keeps him obedient and cringing.

If that doesn't inspire us to question government's licensing of drivers, perhaps the system's inherent insult will. Licensing implies that we are silly children eager to drive without bothering to learn how; only the fatherly State saves us from automotive annihilation.

That paternal motif increasingly characterizes states' interactions with drivers as they withhold this "privilege" to coerce our behavior, the way parents do teens. Many revoke licenses for a long list of infractions, not just those that pertain to driving. Minnesota will suspend a license for "truancy," "underage consumption of alcohol," or merely the "attempt to unlawfully purchase alcohol or tobacco," "failure to pay child support," and "out-of-state conviction." Ohio repeals its permission to drive for "dropping out of high school, drug-related offenses, unsatisfied civil judgments, delinquent, unruly, or habitual drug user (juveniles), failure to appear in court on a bond, liquor law violations, medical condition that would impair your driving ability [and who decides that?], tagged as a 'problem driver' in the National Driver Registry, insurance noncompliance, unresolved out-of-state ticket, out-of-state alcohol- or drug-related offenses."

DMVs not only exploit this authority, they brag about it. "We walk a very fine line with incredible power over people," David Lewis, deputy registrar of the Massachusetts Registry of Motor Vehicles, told author Simson Garfinkel in 1993 for an article published in *Wired Magazine*. Peter Nunnenkamp, manager of driver programs at Oregon's Driver and Motor Vehicle Services agreed. "[Suspending a license is] the most effective thing that you can do without throwing them in jail. . . . And it's fairly cost effective." So much so that DMVs seldom struggle with delinquent debtors. "Last year," Garfinkel wrote, "the Massachusetts Registry collected more than US$660 million in fees and fines; less than $600,000 came back as bounced checks—a whopping 0.1 percent. 'How can you afford to stiff us?' Lewis asks rhetorically. 'Whatever it is you have, we'll take it. We'll pull your driver's license. We'll take your title.'" A capo in the mob sounds less menacing.

Money Is the Real Reason for Licensing

If government were honest enough to say, "Look, we want lots and lots of your money, and we also want to subjugate you," most people would (we hope) deny it the power to license. So as usual, the State cloaks its motives in false solicitude. Licensing protects us, it claims—from selfish sportsmen who would hunt and fish our fields and streams to exhaustion, from broadcasters who would assault our ears with foul language, from reckless drivers. But is any of that true? And if so, if fishermen and radio announcers and drivers are as great a menace as rulers allege, are there more effective ways to protect us from their dangers than by licensing them?

In the case of driver's licenses, the allegations about safety postdate licensing by several decades. Early drivers simply bought licenses without meeting any requirements whatsoever. In fact, folks often ordered them through the mail: no one tested eyesight, competence, or anything else. Only payment received mattered to the issuing government. Carl Watner at *voluntaryist.com* reports that by 1909, "twelve states and the District of Columbia required all automobile drivers to obtain" licenses. These generally listed the operator's "name, address, age, and the type of automobile he claimed to be competent to drive."

That contented many states for years; decades sometimes passed before they also forced drivers to satisfy a bureaucrat as to their vision and skills. Massachusetts and Missouri were both selling licenses by 1903, but only in 1920 did "Massachusetts . . . [pass] its first requirement for an examination of general operators," and "Missouri had no driver examination law until 1952." This at a time when both cars and roads lacked many of the protective features we now take for granted.

DMVs have come a long way since then. Modern ones administer driving and eyesight exams. They harp on seat belts and speed limits. They hang posters about defensive driving in their offices, then compel us to camp out there for hours while slow, surly clerks waste our time and money. That fools most Americans into equating licensed drivers with safe drivers. . . .

Bureaucracy Is the Cause and the Effect

Despite DMVs' propaganda to the contrary, traveling by any means—walking; riding a horse, bus, train, or plane; driving a car—is one of the inalienable rights we possess by virtue of our humanity. Unless we trespass, we assault no one's life, liberty, or property by simply moving from one location to another. The State has no moral authority to interfere.

Why, then, did our grandparents allow government to license cars in the first place? Didn't this strike them as a bizarre and intrusive innovation? After all, no one licensed horses and buggies.

Unfortunately, inventors developed the internal combustion engine just as progressive politics with its veneration of Leviathan [a mythological sea monster used by British philosopher Thomas Hobbes as a metaphor for the political organization of society] was hijacking the nation. Progressives convinced Americans who had formerly distrusted government that it was in fact their best friend, a benign giant protecting them in the frightening, rapidly changing world of electricity, telephones, airplanes, and automobiles.

Add to that the fear most people harbor for new technology, especially technology they can't afford. Cars were playthings for the wealthy when they first appeared on the market—but noisy, smelly nuisances to everyone else. The folks whose horses shied as a newfangled automobile zipped past deeply resented this emerging industry.

And once Mr. Millionaire bought his car, where did he drive it? The early 20th century boasted very few paved roads.

These considerations spurred automotive enthusiasts to welcome government's interest in their hobby. If the State approved of driving enough to license it, everyone must accept it, even those too poor to afford cars. And what politicians regulate, they usually fund, too. The magnates buying horseless carriages wanted all taxpayers, not just themselves, to subsidize the infrastructure their new toys required.

Since then, government has consolidated its conquest of our automotive lives—a conquest so complete most people take it for granted despite the State's incompetence and even criminal negligence. It monopolizes the design and construction of roadways; meanwhile, we mourn roughly 42,000 traffic fatalities year after year. Deliberate carelessness like drunk driving accounts for some of these deaths, but others result when drivers follow the rules of the road as imposed by the State.

Bureaucrats heavily regulate automotive design and manufacture, too. Their latest mania is more miles to the gallon. But many experts blame the requisite flimsiness for more fatalities when crashes occur: cars built from plastic rather than steel reduce consumption of fuel but put occupants at risk. And government's decades of ineptly micromanaging Detroit's Big Three [auto companies] led directly to their failure and nationalization.

In short, an accident of history put government behind the wheel of all things automotive. But there's no reason we should acquiesce in this. Certainly we should work to ensure that PASS ID suffers REAL ID's same fate. But let's go the extra mile and oppose the State's licensing of drivers at all.

Comprehensive Internal Security Database

Whether in their current incarnation or REAL ID's uber-version, driver's licenses swindle huge amounts of our money while giving the State virtually unlimited authority and an excuse for spying on us. They also destroy the private market that would otherwise exist for authenticating one's name and credentials—a market with virtually none of the fraud and identity theft that characterize the government's monopoly of this industry. It would be a differentiated market, too, offering degrees of authentication for everything from cashing a check to entering a restricted area, rather than the one-size-fits-all approach of driver's licenses that divulges our names, addresses, birth-dates, height, and weight to every bank teller and supermarket clerk.

Indeed, frightening amounts of our personal data clog DMVs' computers. Professor Margaret Stock of the United States Military Academy at West Point inadvertently makes that point when arguing that governments should issue driver's licenses to illegal aliens. She writes that "driver license and state identification databases play" a huge "role" "in national security and law enforcement."

"The collective DMV databases are the largest law enforcement databases in the country," she continues, "with records on more individual adults than any other law enforcement databases. The collective DMV databases are the only comprehensive internal security database.

"The Department of Homeland Security (DHS) does not yet have a comprehensive database on all adult residents of the United States. . . . When DHS wants to find someone, the primary government database it relies upon is the driver license database.

"When a person . . . applies for a driver license, that person . . . provides the DMV with a variety of valuable personal information—including a key identifier, the digital photo. DMV databases thus contain biometric information, and a wealth of other valuable information that is updated on a regular basis . . . by the individual who has the license." She insists that other databases can't compete with the depth and breadth of the DMVs'—not the "state birth certificate databases," which record a one-time event without updates, nor the "federal Social Security" and "Internal Revenue Service databases," which lack "biometric information."

Should government know this much about us simply because we drive cars we own on roads we pay for?

Periodical Bibliography

The following articles have been selected to supplement the diverse views presented in this chapter.

Chuck Baldwin   "Homeland Security or Homeland Enslavement?" LewRockwell.com, December 2, 2009. www.lewrockwell.com.

Stanley C. Brubaker   "The Misunderstood Fourth Amendment," *Weekly Standard*, March 6–13, 2006.

Leo Cendrowicz   "Can Airport Body Scanners Stop Terrorist Attacks?" *Time*, January 5, 2010.

Michael Anne Conley   "Your Privacy Matters: Daniel Ellsberg, the USA Patriot Act & You," OpEdNews.com, October 6, 2009. www.opednews.com.

Dave Eberhart   "Privacy, Costs May Be Death of REAL ID Act," *Newsmax*, January 8, 2009.

Economist   "Learning to Live with Big Brother," September 29, 2007.

Froma Harrop   "Terrorist Threat Should Trump Privacy," *Rochester (NY) Democrat and Chronicle*, December 30, 2009. www.democratandchronicle.com.

Michael Humphrey   "Remember Privacy?" *National Catholic Reporter*, November 2, 2007.

Brian Robinson   "Time for a National ID Card?" *Federal Computer Week*, August 21, 2009.

Jacob Sullum   "File Keepers," *Reason*, August 6, 2008.

Olly Zanetti   "You Are Being Watched: Police Surveillance and Intimidation of Political Activists Is Hitting New Heights," *New Internationalist*, June 2009.

OPPOSING
VIEWPOINTS®
SERIES

CHAPTER 2

Do Technological Developments Threaten Privacy?

Chapter Preface

In May 2009, the National Health Interview Survey reported that more than one in five households in America depend solely on cell phones, surpassing those that use only landline phones for the first time. Additionally, one in seven households with landline phones take most or all of their calls on cell phones. The survey estimated that 41 million adults nationwide live in cell-phone-only households.

The technological innovations of cell phones throughout the last decade have made them indispensable in the digital world. They have been used as cameras to capture images and videos of unfolding historical events, such as the 2005 bombings in London and 2009 election protests in Iran. However, these built-in gadgets also pose threats to privacy. For instance, many gyms in Hong Kong banned the use of cell phones in locker rooms. And every 24 Hour Fitness club in the United States posts this sign: "No filming, videotaping, or photography is permitted in the club without the written permission of management."[1]

The addition of Global Positioning System (GPS) chips to cell phones is also a double-edge sword. It can guide lost drivers and travelers to their destinations, and services like Accu-Tracking and Guardian Angel Technology allow adults to track their children in real-time when they carry wireless devices. But such applications can be used to invade privacy, critics say. "A jealous husband could give his wife a cell phone with tracking already enabled," contends Andrew Brandt, senior associate editor at *PC World*. "Police might try to obtain tracking data for an investigation, or just to issue speeding tickets after the fact."[2] Brandt acknowledges that GPS can be disabled

1. Quoted in Elisa Batista, "New Privacy Menace: Cell Phones?" *Wired*, February 17, 2003. www.wired.com/techbiz/media/news/2003/02/57692.
2. Andrew Brandt, "Privacy Watch: Soon, Your Cell Phone May Be Tracking You," *PC World*, February 25, 2004. www.pcworld.com/article/114721/privacy_watch_soon_your_cell_phone_may_be_tracking_you.html.

in cell phones, but that many users are unaware of such settings. In the following chapter, the authors debate how emerging technologies may make us more vulnerable or secure.

> *"In this environment, the real problem is not that your information is out there; it's that it's not protected from misuse."*

Internet Privacy Can Be Protected

Simson Garfinkel

In the following viewpoint, Simson Garfinkel claims that online privacy is possible in a technological world. While abstinence from electronic transactions and computers cannot wholly protect an individual's privacy, Garfinkel advocates user awareness and better security practices and policies. For instance, he contends that businesses and institutions can work harder to prevent data theft and advanced programs can solve common computer vulnerabilities. Garfinkel also recommends the creation of a single electronic identification system through linking state-issued identification to a user's Internet activities. The author is an associate professor at the Naval Postgraduate School in Monterey, California.

Simson Garfinkel, "Privacy Requires Security, Not Abstinence: Protecting an Inalienable Right in the Age of Facebook," *Technology Review*, vol. 112, July–August, 2009, pp. 64, 66–68, 70–72. Copyright © 2009 by the Association of Alumni and Alumnae of MIT. Reproduced by permission.

As you read, consider the following questions:

1. How does Garfinkel support his position that opting out of using modern-day technologies does not guarantee privacy?

2. Why do privacy activists use Facebook, in Garfinkel's view?

3. According to Garfinkel, how would enabling the use of state-issued IDs online protect privacy?

Privacy matters. Data privacy protects us from electronic crimes of opportunity—identity theft, stalking, even little crimes like spam. Privacy gives us the right to meet and speak confidentially with others—a right that's crucial for democracy, which requires places for political ideas to grow and mature. Absolute privacy, also known as solitude, gives us no space to grow as individuals. Who could learn to write, draw, or otherwise create if every action, step, and misstep were captured, immortalized, and evaluated? And the ability to conduct transactions in privacy protects us from both legal and illegal discrimination.

Until recently, people who wanted to preserve their privacy were urged to "opt out" or abstain from some aspects of modern society. Concerned about having your purchases tracked by a credit-card company? Use cash. Concerned that E-ZPass records might be used against you in a lawsuit? Throw coins at that toll booth. Don't want to show your ID at the airport? Drive. Don't want your location tracked minute by minute? Turn off your cell phone. And be in a minority: faced with the choice of convenience or privacy, Americans have overwhelmingly chosen the former. Companies like TJX [discount retail chains that include TJMaxx and Marshalls] haven't even suffered from allowing their customers' personal data to be leaked.

Now, however, abstinence no longer guarantees privacy. Of course, it never really did. But until the past two decades it was always possible to keep some private information out of circulation. Today, although you can avoid the supermarket savings card, the market will still capture your face with its video cameras. You can use cash, but large cash transactions are reported to the federal government. You can try to live without the Internet—but you'll be marginalized. Worse, you won't be able to participate in the public debate about how your privacy is wasting away—because that debate is happening online. And no matter what you do, it won't prevent your information from being stored in commercial networked systems.

Security Needs to Be a Priority

In this environment, the real problem is not that your information is out there; it's that it's not protected from misuse. In other words, privacy problems are increasingly the result of poor security practices. The biggest issue, I've long maintained, is that decision makers don't consider security a priority. By not insisting on secure systems, governments and corporations alike have allowed themselves to get stuck with insecure ones.

Consider the humble Social Security number [SSN]. As a privacy advocate, I always chafe when people ask me for my "social." As a security professional, I am deeply disturbed that a number designed as an identifier—for the single specific purpose of tracking individuals' earnings to calculate Social Security benefits—has come to be used as a verifier of identity for countless other purposes. Providing my SSN should not "prove" that I am who I say I am any more than providing my name or address does. But in the absence of any better system, this number has become, in the words of Joanne McNabb, chief of California's Office of Privacy Protection, the "key to the vault for identity thieves."

71

Yes, privacy as we know it is under attack—by a government searching for tax cheats and terrorists; by corporations looking for new customers; by insurance companies looking to control costs; and even by nosy friends, associates, and classmates. Collectively, we made things worse by not building strong privacy and security guarantees into our information systems, our businesses, and our society. Then we went and networked everything, helping both legitimate users and criminals. Is it any wonder things turned out this way?

All of a sudden, we have a lot of work to do.

But while our current privacy issues feel as new as Twitter, the notion of privacy as a right is old. Americans have always expected this right to be maintained, even as technology opened ever more powerful tools for its subversion. The story of privacy in America is the story of inventions and the story of fear; it is best told around certain moments of opportunity and danger.

The Constitution Does Protect Privacy

The word *privacy* doesn't appear in the U.S. Constitution, but courts and constitutional scholars have found plenty of privacy protections in the restriction on quartering soldiers in private homes (the Third Amendment); in the prohibition against "unreasonable searches and seizures" (the Fourth Amendment); and in the prohibition against forcing a person to be "a witness against himself" (the Fifth Amendment). These provisions remain fundamental checks on the power of government.

Over time, however, the advance of technology has threatened privacy in new ways, and the way we think about the concept has changed accordingly.

Back in 1890 two Boston lawyers, Samuel Warren and Louis Brandeis, wrote an article in the *Harvard Law Review* warning that the invasive technologies of their day threatened to take "what is whispered in the closet" and have it "proclaimed from the house-tops." In the face of those threats, they posited a direct "right to privacy" and argued that individuals whose privacy is violated should be able to sue for damages.

Warren and Brandeis called privacy "the right to be let alone" and gave numerous examples of ways it could be invaded. After more than a century of legal scholarship, we've come to understand that these examples suggest four distinct kinds of invasion: intrusion into a person's seclusion or private affairs; disclosure of embarrassing private facts; publicity that places a person in a "false light"; and appropriation of a person's name or likeness.

In our world, "intrusions into a person's seclusion or private affairs" might describe someone's hacking into your computer system. Consider the case of Patrick Connolly, a U.S. military contractor accused of victimizing more than 4,000 teenagers by breaking into their computers and threatening to make their pictures and videos public unless they sent him sexually explicit photos and videos of themselves. You can also be intruded upon in many lesser ways: when companies force advertisements onto your screen, for example, or make pop-ups appear that you need to close. It's intrusive for a telemarketer to call you during dinner. That's why programs that block Internet advertisements and the federal government's "do not call" list are both rightly seen as privacy-protecting measures.

The desire to prevent the disclosure of embarrassing private facts, meanwhile, is one of the driving forces behind the privacy regulations of the Health Insurance Portability and Accountability Act (HIPAA). Because of this law and the regulations deriving from it, a health-care provider cannot disclose information in your medical records unless you give explicit permission. Another law, the Video Privacy Protection Act of 1988, makes it illegal for Netflix to disclose the movies you rent.

The Law and Online Privacy Issues

"False light" is a problem we still don't know how to address online. It's all too easy on today's Internet to attack a person's reputation with anonymously posted false statements. And even though free-speech advocates invariably say that the anti-dote to bad speech is more speech, experience has shown that this remedy is less effective in the age of Google. For example, two years ago AutoAdmit, an online message board for law students and lawyers, was sued by two female Yale Law students who said they'd been unable to obtain summer associate positions because vile and malicious sexual comments about them appeared whenever someone searched for their names.

Using a name or likeness without permission is at the heart of most "sexting" cases that reach the newspapers. Journalists often focus on the fact that teens are willingly sending sexy or downright pornographic photos of themselves to their boyfriends or girlfriends. But the real damage happens when a recipient forwards one of these photos to friends. That is, the damage is caused by the appropriation, not the receipt.

The fact that a dusty *Harvard Law Review* article corresponds so closely with the online privacy problems we face today suggests that even though technology is a driving factor in these privacy invasions, it's not the root source. The source is what sits in front of the computer's screen, not behind it. . . .

Computers and Internet Brought Changes

Consumer data banks as we know them today—big repositories of personal information, indexed by name and specifically constructed for the purpose of sharing information once regarded as "private"—didn't start with computers. But computers certainly helped. . . .

In the 1980s and early 1990s, while lawmakers in Europe and Canada passed comprehensive privacy legislation complete with commissioners and enforcement mechanisms, the United States adopted a piecemeal approach [to computerized data banks]. Some databases had legally mandated privacy guarantees; others didn't. Wiretapping required a warrant—except when companies taped employees for the purpose of "improving customer service." But even if policies weren't consistent, they basically covered most situations that arose.

Then came the Internet's explosive growth—a boon to community, commerce, and surveillance all at the same time. Never before had it been so easy to find out so much, so quickly. But while most Internet users soon became dependent on services from companies like Yahoo and Google, few realized that they themselves were the product these companies were selling.

All activity on the Internet is mediated—by software on your computer and on the remote service; by the remote service itself; and by the Internet service providers [ISPs] that carry the data. Each of these mediators has the ability to record or change the data as it passes through. And each mediator has an incentive to exploit its position for financial gain.

Unauthorized Information Sharing

Thousands of different business models bloomed. Companies like Doubleclick realized that they could keep track of which Internet users went to which websites and integrate this information into vast profiles of user preferences, to be used for targeting ads. Some ISPs went further and inserted their own advertisements into the user's data stream. One e-mail provider went further still: it intercepted all the e-mail from *Amazon.com* to its users and used those messages to market its own online clearinghouse for rare and out-of-print books. Woops. That provider was eventually charged with violating the Federal Wiretap Act. But practically every other intrusive practice was allowed by the law and, ultimately, by Congress, which was never able to muster the will to pass comprehensive Internet privacy legislation.

It's not that Congress was shy about regulating the Internet. It's just that congressional attention in the 1990s was focused on shielding children from online pornography—through laws eventually found unconstitutional by the Supreme Court, because they also limited the rights of adults. The one significant piece of Internet privacy legislation that Congress did manage to pass was the Children's Online Privacy Protection Act (COPPA), which largely prohibited the intentional collection of information from children 12 or younger.

Instead, it fell mostly to the Federal Trade Commission [FTC] to regulate privacy on the Internet. And here the commission used one primary tool: the FTC Act of 1914 (since updated), which prohibits businesses from engaging in "unfair or deceptive acts or practices." The way this works in connection with online privacy is that companies write "privacy policies" describing what they do with personal information they obtain from their customers. Companies that follow their policies are fine—even if they collect your information and publish it, sell it, or use it to send e-mail or for "any other lawful purpose" (and the law is pretty tolerant). The only way for companies to get in trouble is to claim that they will honor your privacy in a specific manner and then do something different. . . .

Does Facebook Allow Unlimited Access?

Originally conceived as a place for Harvard undergraduates to post their photos and cell-phone numbers—information that Harvard, because of privacy concerns, wasn't putting online back in 2003—Facebook has grown to be the fourth-most-popular "website" in the world, according to the Web services firm Alexa. But Facebook is really a collection of applications powered by private information: a smart address book that friends and business contacts update themselves; a (mostly) spam-free messaging system; a photo-sharing site. And on Facebook, developers write seamlessly integrated applications.

These applications are troubling from a privacy perspective. Say you want to complete one of those cool Facebook surveys. Click a button and you'll be taken to a page with the headline "Allow Access?" Then you'll be told that using the application allows it to "pull your profile information, photos, your friends' info, and other content that it requires to work." How much information? There's no way to be sure, really—perhaps everything you've put into Facebook.

The roughly one in five Internet users who spend an average of 25 minutes each day on Facebook implicitly face a question every time they type into a Facebook page: Do they trust the site's security and privacy controls? The answer is inevitably yes.

That's the reason privacy activists are on Facebook: it's where the action is. It's easy to imagine a future where most personal messaging is done on such platforms. Activists and organizations that refuse to take part might find themselves irrelevant.

It was in a similar context that Scott McNealy, then CEO [chief executive officer] of Sun Microsystems, famously said, "You have zero privacy anyway. Get over it." In January 1999, McNealy was trying to promote a new technology for distributed computing that Sun had cooked up—an early version of what we might call "cloud computing" today—and reporters were pestering him about how the system would protect privacy. Four and a half years later, he told the *San Francisco Chronicle*, "The point I was making was someone already has your medical records. Someone has my dental records. Someone has my financial records. Someone knows just about everything about me."

Today it's not just medical and financial records that are stored on remote servers—it's everything. Consider e-mail. If you download it from Post Office Protocol (POP) accounts, as most Internet users still did in 1999, the mail is copied to your computer and then deleted from your ISP's servers. These days, however, most people use Web mail or the Internet Message Access Protocol (IMAP), which leaves a copy on the server until it is explicitly deleted. Most people don't know where that server is—it's just somewhere "in the cloud" of the Internet.

Services like Facebook, Gmail, and Google Docs are becoming wildly popular because they give users the freedom to access their data from home and from work without having to carry it back and forth. But leaving your data on some organization's servers creates all sorts of opportunities for mishap. The organization might have a bad employee who siphons out data for personal profit. Cyberthieves might break into its servers and try to steal lots of people's data at the same time. Or a hacker might specifically target your data and contact the organization, claiming to be you. All these are security threats—security threats that become privacy threats because it's your data.

Where We Are Now

I have spent a good part of my professional life looking for ways to make computer systems more secure, and I believe that many of the problems we face today are not only tractable—many of them have already been solved. The threat of data theft by insiders can be mitigated by paying employees enough, auditing their work, limiting the amount of authority that any one employee has, and harshly punishing any individual who abuses the employer's trust. Computer systems can be made immune to buffer-overflow attacks [which force data into external, potentially unprotected, storage space], one of the most common security vulnerabilities in recent years, by programming them in modern languages like Java and Python instead of 1980s standards like C and C++. We really do know how to build secure systems. Unfortunately, these systems cost more to develop, and using them would require us to abandon the ones we already have—at least for our critical applications.

You Can Opt Out of Sharing Your Personal Information

Most Web sites now have privacy policies that describe what kind of information the site collects from you, how it is stored and used, and who it is shared with. However, just because a site has something called a "Privacy Policy" does not mean that the site protects your privacy. On the contrary, often buried in the dense language of "privacy policies" are broad statements that your information will be disclosed to third parties and used for a variety of purposes. . . .

As you sign-up for accounts with online merchants and social networking sites, pay particular attention to the various privacy settings and privacy options offered to you. For example, many online companies provide you with the option to get off or "opt-out" of the lists that share your information. A number of companies go a step further and ask your permission ("opt-in") before sharing personal information that they collect. Brand name companies will respect your choices. Too often, however, companies make opting out difficult, so you may have to dig through their privacy policy to find where to opt-out.

Center for Democracy & Technology,
"CDT's Guide to Online Privacy: Tips,"
October 27, 2009. www.cdt.org.

But one fundamental problem is harder to solve: identifying people on the Internet. What happens if somebody impersonating you calls up a company and demands access to your data?

If Google or Yahoo were storefronts, they would ask to see a state-issued ID card. They might compare a photo of you that they took when you opened the account with the person now standing in their lobby. Yes, there are phony IDs, and there are scams. Nevertheless, identification technology works pretty well most of the time in the physical world.

It turns out that we essentially have the technology to solve this problem in the digital world as well. Yet the solutions that have been developed aren't politically tenable—not only because of perceived costs but also, ironically, because of perceived privacy concerns.

I understand these fears, but I think they are misplaced. When someone can wreak havoc by misappropriating your personal data, privacy is threatened far more by the lack of a reliable online identification system than it would be by the introduction of one. And it is likely that it would cost society far more money to live with poor security than to address it.

I believe that we will be unable to protect online privacy without a strong electronic identity system that's free to use and backed by the governments of the world—a true passport for online access. One of the fundamental duties of government is to protect the internal security of the nation so that commerce can take place. For hundreds of years, that has meant creating identification documents so that people can prove their citizenship and their identity. But the U.S. government has abdicated its responsibility in the online world, and businesses have made up their own systems—like asking for your Social Security number and address, and perhaps your favorite color.

The difficulty of identifying people in the electronic world is a problem for every single company, every single organization, every single website. And it is especially a problem for Facebook and Google, because at a very basic level, they don't know who their customers are. When you open an account at a bank, U.S. law requires that you prove your identity with some state-issued identification. Bank accounts are linked to an actual identity. But electronic accounts like those on Facebook and Google aren't. They project an identity, but they aren't linked, really, to anything. That's a real problem if some hacker takes over your Gmail account and you need to get it back.

Modern Policies Can Protect Internet Privacy

One solution would be to make driver's licenses and other state-issued IDs usable online by adding electronic chips. Just imagine: no more passwords to access your bank account, to buy something at *Amazon*, or to bid on *eBay*. Just insert your card. And if you lost the card, you could report it missing and get a new one. Instantly, all your online accounts would recognize the new credential and refuse to honor the old one. . . .

Though a stronger identification system would undoubtedly harm some citizens through errors, I think the opposition is unfortunate. We're already being identified every time we use an online banking service, or make an online purchase, or even use Facebook. We're just being identified through ad hoc, broken systems that are easy for bad guys to exploit. If we had a single strong identity system, we could adopt legislation to protect it from inappropriate use. A California law enacted in 2003, for example, prevents bars, car dealers, and others from collecting information swiped from a driver's license for any purpose other than age verification or license authentication.

For more than 100 years, American jurisprudence has recognized privacy as a requirement for democracy, social relations, and human dignity. For nearly 50, we've understood that protecting privacy takes more than just controlling intrusions into your home; it also requires being able to control information about you that's available to businesses, government, and society at large. Even though Americans were told after 9/11 that we needed to choose between security and privacy, it's increasingly clear that without one we will never have the other.

We need to learn how to protect privacy by intention, not by accident. Although technology can help, my belief is that such protections need to start with clearly articulated policies. Just as [President Richard] Nixon created the Environmental Protection Agency to protect our environment, we need some kind of Privacy Protection Agency to give our rights a fighting chance. Our piecemeal approach is no longer acceptable.

> *"Digital systems have virtually eliminated a simple privacy that many people take for granted in daily life: the idea that there can be anonymity in a crowd."*

Internet Privacy Is Imperiled

Jonathan Shaw

In the following viewpoint, Jonathan Shaw states that privacy on the Internet is in danger. He warns that identifying information and financial records can be culled from Web sites, and Social Security numbers can be determined from Internet users' social-networking profiles. Electronic purchases, databases of medical and police records, and online activity, Shaw continues, also threaten anonymity. While the Internet has its benefits, the author advises that privacy be protected and user confidence assured through better online tools and regulations. Shaw is the managing editor of Harvard Magazine, *a periodical for Harvard University alumni, faculty, and staff.*

As you read, consider the following questions:

1. As told by Shaw, why are many Facebook users at risk of having their Social Security numbers stolen?

Jonathan Shaw, "Exposed: The Erosion of Privacy in the Internet Era," *Harvard Magazine,* September–October 2009. Copyright © 2009 Harvard Magazine Inc. Reproduced by permission.

2. Why is data transmitted over wireless networks in the clear, according to Shaw?

3. In Emily Nussbaum's opinion, how do young people view privacy?

Imagine if you waved to someone and, without your knowledge, a high-resolution camera took a photograph of your hand, capturing your fingerprints. You might be upset. Or—if you were visiting Disneyland, where they already make an image of your fingerprint to save you from waiting in a long line—you might find the novelty of the technology, and the immediate benefits ... gratifying. The ambivalence we sometimes feel about new technologies that reveal identifiable personal information balances threats to privacy against incremental advantages. Indisputably, the trends toward miniaturization and mass-market deployment of cameras, recording devices, low-power sensors, and medical monitors of all kinds—when combined with the ability to digitally collect, store, retrieve, classify, and sort very large amounts of information—offer many benefits, but also threaten civil liberties and expectations of personal privacy. George Orwell's vision in [his novel] *1984* of a future in which the government has the power to record everything seems not so farfetched. "But even Orwell did not imagine that the sensors would be things that everybody would have," says [Harvard University's] McKay professor of computer science Harry Lewis. "He foresaw the government putting the cameras on the lampposts—which we have. He didn't foresee the 14-year-old girl snapping pictures on the T [the Boston-area subway system]. Or the fact that flash drives that are given away as party favors could carry crucial data on everybody in the country."

It's a Smaller World

Information technology changes the accessibility and presentation of information. Lewis gives talks on the subject of privacy to alumni groups in private homes, and often begins with an example that puts his hosts on the hot seat. He projects a Google Earth view of the house, then shows the website *Zillow*'s assessment of how much it is worth, how many bedrooms and bathrooms and square feet it has. Then he goes to *fundrace.huffingtonpost.com*, an interface to the Federal Elections Commission's campaign-contributions database. "Such information has always been a matter of public record," says Lewis, "but it used to be that you had to go somewhere and give the exact name and address and they would give you back the one piece of data. Now you can just mouse over your neighborhood and little windows pop up and show how much money all the neighbors have given." In the 02138 zip code, you can see "all the Harvard faculty members who gave more than $1,000 to Barack Obama," for example. "This seems very invasive," says Lewis, "but in fact it is the opposite of an invasion of privacy: it is something that our elected representatives decided should be public."

Technology has forced people to rethink the public/private distinction. "Now it turns out that there is private, public, and *really, really* public," Lewis says. "We've effectively said that anyone in an Internet café in Nairobi should be able to see how much our house is worth." Lewis has been blogging about such issues on the website *www.bitsbook.com*, a companion to *Blown to Bits: Your Life, Liberty, and Happiness after the Digital Explosion*, the 2008 book of which he is a coauthor. "We think because we have a word for privacy that it is something we can put our arms around," he says. "But it's not."

One of the best attempts to define the full range of privacy concerns at their intersection with new technologies, "A Taxonomy of Privacy," appeared in the *University of Pennsylvania Law Review* in 2006. Its author, Daniel Solove, now a professor at George Washington University Law School, identified 16 privacy harms modulated by new technologies, including: information collection by surveillance; aggregation of information; insecurity of information; and disclosure, exposure, distortion, and increased accessibility of information.

That privacy would be a concern of the legal profession is not surprising. What *is* surprising is that computer scientists have been in the vanguard of those seeking ways to protect privacy, partly because they are often the first to recognize privacy problems engendered by new technologies and partly because the solutions themselves are sometimes technological. At Harvard, the Center for Research on Computation and Society (CRCS) has become a focal point for such inquiry. CRCS, which brings computer scientists together with colleagues from other schools and academic disciplines, was founded to develop new ideas and technologies for addressing some of society's most vexing problems, and prides itself on a forward-looking, integrative approach. Privacy and security have been a particular focus during the past few years.

Database linking offers one such area of concern. If you tell Latanya Sweeney, A.L.B. [bachelor of liberal arts, Harvard] '95, nothing about yourself except your birth date and five-digit zip code, she'll tell you your name. If you are under the age of 30 and tell her where you were born, she can correctly predict eight or nine digits of your nine-digit Social Security number. "The main reason privacy is a growing problem is that disk storage is so cheap," says [Sweeney, now a] visiting professor of computer science, technology, and policy at CRCS. "People can collect data and never throw anything away. Policies on data sharing are not very good, and the result is that data tend to flow around and get linked to other data. . . ."

Private Information Is Easily Gathered

A potentially even more serious privacy crisis looms in the way Social Security numbers (SSNs) are assigned, Sweeney says. "We are entering a situation where a huge number of people could tell me just their date of birth and hometown, and I can predict their SSN. Why is this a problem? Because in order to apply for a credit card, the key things I need are your name, your date of birth, your address, and your SSN. Who is the population at risk? Young people on Facebook."

Facebook asks for your date of birth and hometown, two pieces of information that most young people include on their pages simply because they want their friends to wish them a happy birthday. The problem is that SSNs have never been issued randomly—the first three digits are a state code, the second two are assigned by region within state—and the process is described on a public website of the Social Security Administration. Starting in 1980, when the Internal Revenue Service began requiring that children have SSNs to be claimed as dependents on their parents' tax returns, the numbers started being assigned at birth. Thus, if you know a person's date and location of birth, it becomes increasingly simple to predict the SSN.

One way or another, says Sweeney, someone is going to exploit this privacy crisis, and it "is either going to become a disaster or we'll circumvent it." (Canada and New Zealand, she notes, may have similar problems.) "But there are many easy remedies," she adds. She has proposed random assignment of SSNs from a central repository. She has also devised solutions for setting up public-health surveillance systems that don't reveal personal information, but still work as early-warning systems for infectious-disease transmission or bioterror attacks.

Sweeney believes that technological approaches to privacy problems are often better than legislative solutions, because "you don't lose the benefits of the technology." One of her current projects, for example, aims to make sure that technologies like photographic fingerprint capture are implemented in such a way that personal privacy is maintained and individuals' rights aren't exposed to abuse.

Scientists have long been excited by the possibilities of using biometric information such as fingerprints, palmprints, or iris scans for positive identification: people could use them to open their cars or their homes. But just how private are fingerprints? With a grant from the National Institutes of Justice, Sweeney and her students have shown that inexpensive digital cameras are already good enough to capture fingertip friction-ridge information at a range of two to three feet, and image resolution and capture speed are improving all the time, even as the cost of the technology keeps dropping. As a result, because it is contactless and very cheap, photographic fingerprint capture could become "the dominant way that prints are captured in a lot of public spaces," Sweeney explains. That means fingerprint databases are everywhere, and "you don't have any control over the use of those prints, if somebody wanted to make a false print, or track you. It is like walking around with your Social Security number on your forehead, to an extent. It is a little different because it isn't linked to your credit report or your credit card"—but it does not require a tremendous leap of imagination to picture a world where credit cards require fingerprint verification. . . .

A Legal Privacy Patchwork

As the Facebook/SSN interaction and the ability to capture fingerprints with digital photography illustrate, social changes mediated by technology alter the context in which privacy is protected. But privacy laws have not kept up. The last burst of widespread public concern about privacy came in the 1970s, when minicomputers and mainframes predominated. The government was the main customer, and fear that the government would know everything about its citizens led to the passage of the Privacy Act of 1974. That law set the standard on fair information practices for ensuing legislation in Europe and Canada—but in the United States, the law was limited to circumscribing what information the *government* could collect; it didn't apply to commercial enterprises like credit-card companies. No one imagined today's situation, when you can be tracked by your cell phone, your laptop, or another wireless device. As for ATM [automated teller machine] transactions and credit-card purchases, Sweeney says "pretty much everything is being recorded on some database somewhere."

The result is that even the 1974 law has been undermined, says CRCS postdoctoral fellow Allan Friedman, because it "does not address the government *buying* information from *private* actors. This is a massive loophole, because private actors are much better at gathering information anyway."

As new privacy concerns surfaced in American life, legislators responded with a finger-in-the-dike mentality, a "patchwork" response, Friedman continues. "The great example of this is that for almost 10 years, your video-rental records had stronger privacy protection than either your financial or your medical records." The video-rental records law—passed in 1988 after a newspaper revealed Supreme Court nominee Robert Bork's rentals—was so narrowly crafted that most people think it doesn't even apply to Netflix. "Bork didn't have much to hide," Friedman says, "but clearly enough people in Congress did." Medical records were protected under the Health Insurance Portability and Accountability Act in 1996, but financial records weren't protected until the Gramm-Leach-Bliley Act of 1999. (Student records are protected by the Family Educational Rights and Privacy Act, passed in 1974, while the Children's Online Privacy Protection Act, passed 1998, prohibits the online collection of personal information from children under the age of 13.) "Legally," Friedman concludes, "privacy in this country is a mishmash based on the common-law tradition. We don't have a blanket regulation to grant us protection," as Europe does.

The End of Anonymity

Friedman co-taught a new undergraduate course on the subject of privacy last year [2008]; it covered topics ranging from public policy and research ethics to wiretapping and database anonymity. "If there is a unified way to think about what digital systems have done to privacy," he says, it is that they collapse contexts: social, spatial, temporal, and financial. "If I pay my credit-card bill late, I understand the idea that it will affect a future credit-card decision," he explains: "But I don't want to live in a society where I have to think, 'Well, if I use my card in this establishment, that will change my creditworthiness in the future'"—a reference to a recent *New York Times Magazine* story, "What Does Your Credit-Card Company Know about You?" It reported that a Canadian credit-card issuer had discovered that people who used their card in a particular pool hall in Montreal, for example, had a 47 percent chance of missing four payments during the subsequent 12 months, whereas people who bought birdseed or anti-scuff felt pads for the legs of their furniture almost never missed payments. These disaggregated bits of information turn out to be better predictors of creditworthiness than traditional measures, but their use raises concerns, Friedman points out: "We don't know how our information is being used to make decisions about us."

Take the case of someone with a venereal disease who doesn't want the people in his social network to know. "If I go to the hospital and the nurse who sees me happens to live down the street," says Friedman, "maybe I don't want her peeking at my medical records." That particular threat has always been there in charts, he notes, but problems like this scale up dramatically with online systems. Now the nurse could check the records of everyone on her street during a coffee break. He cites a related example: "Massachusetts has a single State Police records system and there have been tens of thousands of lookups for Tom Brady and other local sports stars." Unlike celebrities, ordinary people have not had to worry about such invasions of privacy in the past, but now computers can be used to find needles in haystacks—virtually every time. There are nearly seven billion people on the planet: a big number for a human brain, but a small number for a computer to scan. "John Smith is fairly safe," says Friedman, "unless you know something critical about John Smith, and then all of a sudden, it is easy to find him."

Digital systems have virtually eliminated a simple privacy that many people take for granted in daily life: the idea that there can be anonymity in a crowd. Computer scientists often refer to a corollary of this idea: security through obscurity. "If you live in a house, you might leave your door unlocked," Friedman says. "The chances that someone is going to try your front door are fairly small. But I think you have to lock your door if you live in an apartment building. What digital systems do is allow someone to pry and test things very cheaply. And they can test a lot of doors."

He notes that computers running the first version of Windows XP will be discovered *and* hacked, on average, in less than four minutes, enabling the criminal to take control of the system without the owner's consent or knowledge. Botnets—networks of machines that have been taken over—find vulnerable systems through brute force, by testing every address on the Internet, a sobering measure of the scale of such attacks. (Another measure: the CEO [chief executive officer] of AT&T recently testified before Congress that Internet crime costs an estimated $1 trillion annually. That is clearly an overestimate, says Friedman, but nobody knows how much Internet crime actually *does* cost, because there are no disclosure requirements for online losses, even in the banking industry.)

The durability of data represents another kind of contextual collapse. "Knowing whether something is harmful now versus whether it will be harmful in the future is tricky," Friedman notes. "A canonical example occurred in the 1930s, when intellectuals in some circles might have been expected to attend socialist gatherings. Twenty years later," during the McCarthy era, "this was a bad piece of information to have floating around." Friedman wonders what will happen when young bloggers with outspoken opinions today start running for political office. How will their earlier words be used against them? Will they be allowed to change their minds?

Access Is Too Easy

Because personal information is everywhere, inevitably it leaks. Friedman cites the research of former CRCS fellow Simson Garfinkel, now an associate of the School of Engineering and Applied Sciences and associate professor at the Naval Postgraduate School, who reported in 2003 that fully one-third of 1,000 used hard drives he had purchased on eBay and at swap meets still contained sensitive financial information. One that had been part of an ATM machine was loaded with thousands of credit-card numbers, as was another that a supermarket had used to transmit credit-card payments to its bank. Neither had been properly "wiped" of its data.

Data insecurity is not just accidental, however. *Most* Web-based data transmitted over wireless networks is sent "in the clear," unencrypted. Anyone using the same network can intercept and read it. (Google is the only major Web-based e-mail provider that offers encryption, but as of this writing, users must hunt for the option to turn it on.) Harry Lewis smiled at the naiveté of the question when asked what software the laptop used to write this article would need to intercept e-mails or other information at a Starbucks, for example. "Your computer is all set up to do it, and there are a million free 'packet sniffers' you can download to make it easy," he said. And the risk that somebody might detect this illegal surveillance? "Zero, unless somebody looks at your screen and sees what you are doing," because the packet sniffers passively record airborne data, giving out no signals of their presence.

Civil libertarians are more concerned that the government can easily access electronic communications because the data are centralized, passing through a relatively few servers owned by companies that can legally be forced to allow surveillance without public disclosure. Noting that the conversation tends to end whenever privacy is pitted against national-security interests, Friedman nevertheless asks, "Do we want to live in a society where the government can—regardless of whether they use the power or not—have access to all of our communications? So that they can, if they feel the need, drill down and find us?"

Social Changes

Paralleling changes in the way digital systems compromise our security are the evolving social changes in attitudes toward privacy. How much do we really value it? As Lewis points out, "We'll give away data on our purchasing habits for a 10-cent discount on a bag of potato chips." But mostly, he says, "people don't really know what they want. They'll say one thing and then do something else."

Noting young people's willingness to post all kinds of personal information on social networking sites such as Facebook—including photographs that might compromise them later—some commentators have wondered if there has been a generational shift in attitudes toward privacy. In "Say Everything," a February 2007 *New York Magazine* article, author Emily Nussbaum noted:

> Younger people . . . are the only ones for whom it seems to have sunk in that the idea of a truly private life is already an illusion. Every street in New York has a surveillance camera. Each time you swipe your debit card at Duane Reed or use your MetroCard, that transaction is tracked. Your employer owns your e-mails. The NSA [National Security Agency] owns your phone calls. Your life is being lived in public whether you choose to acknowledge it or not. . . . So it may be time to consider the possibility that young people who behave as if privacy doesn't exist are actually the sane people, not the insane ones.

Some bloggers, noting that our hunter-gatherer ancestors would have lived communally, have even suggested that privacy may be an anomalous notion, a relatively recent histori-cal invention that might again disappear. "My response to that," says Lewis, "is that, yes, it happened during the same few years in history that are associated with the whole devel-opment of individual rights, the empowerment of individuals, and the rights of the individual against government authori-ties. That is a notion that is tied up, I think, with the notion of a right to privacy. So it is worrisome to me."

Nor is it the case that young people don't care about pri-vacy, says danah boyd, a fellow at the Law School's Berkman Center for Internet and Society who studies how youth engage with social media. "Young people care deeply about privacy, but it is a question of control, not what information gets out there," she explains. "For a lot of teenagers, the home has never been a private place. They feel they have more control on a service like Facebook or MySpace than they do at home."

She calls this not a generational difference, but a life-stage difference. Adults, boyd says, understand context in terms of physical space. They may go out to a pub on Friday night with friends, but not with their boss. For young people, online contexts come just as naturally, and many, she has found, ac-tually share their social network passwords with other friends as a token of trust or intimacy (hence the analogy to a safe space like a pub).

Teens *do* realize that someone other than their friends may access this personal information. "They understand the col-lapse of social context, but may decide that status among their peers is more important," she notes. "But do they understand that things like birth dates can be used by entities beyond their visibility? No. Most of them are barely aware that they have a Social Security number. But should they be the ones trying to figure this out, or do we really need to rethink our privacy structures around our identity information and our fi-nancial information?

"My guess," boyd continues, "is that the kinds of systems we have set up—which assume a certain kind of obscurity of basic data—won't hold going into the future. We need to rethink how we do identity assessment for credit cards and bank accounts and all of that, and then to try to convince people not to give out their birth dates."

Friedman agrees that financial information needs to be handled differently. Why, he asks, is a credit record always open for a new line of credit by default, enabling fraud to happen at any time? "Is it because the company that maintains the record gets a fee for each credit check?" (Security freezes on a person's credit report are put in place only ex post facto in cases of identity theft at the request of the victim.) Friedman believes that the best way to fight widespread distribution and dissemination of personal information is with better transparency, because that affords individuals and policymakers a better understanding of the risks involved.

"You don't necessarily want to massively restrict information-sharing, because a lot of it is voluntary and beneficial," he explains. Privacy, in the simplest of terms, is about *context* of information sharing, rather than *control* of information sharing: "It is about allowing me to determine what kind of environment I am in, allowing me to feel confident in expressing myself in that domain, without having it spill over into another. That encompasses everything from giving my credit-card number to a company—and expecting them to use it securely and for the intended purpose only—to Facebook and people learning not to put drunk pictures of themselves online." Some of this will have to be done through user empowerment—giving users better tools—and some through regulation. "We do need to revisit the Privacy Act of 1974," he says. "We do need to have more information about who has information about us and who is buying that information, even if we don't have control."

There is always the possibility that we will decide as a society not to support privacy. Harry Lewis believes that would be society's loss. "I think ultimately what you lose is the development of individual identity," he says. "The more we are constantly exposed from a very young age to peer and other social pressure for our slightly aberrant behaviors, the more we tend to force ourselves, or have our parents force us, into social conformity. So the loss of privacy is kind of a regressive force. Lots of social progress has been made because a few people tried things under circumstances where they could control who knew about them, and then those communities expanded, and those new things became generally accepted, often not without a fight. With the loss of privacy, there is some threat to that spirit of human progress through social experimentation."

> "Cameras, when properly used and
> monitored, can be one of many weap-
> ons in our arsenal against crime."

Public Video Surveillance
Can Enhance Safety

J. Richard Gray

*In the following viewpoint, excerpted from his statement before
the Lancaster, Pennsylvania, Safety Commission, J. Richard Gray
claims that public video surveillance can aid law enforcement
and make communities safer. But he insists that several factors
must be reviewed if security cameras are installed in public areas: the preservation of privacy, potential of abuses, and objections of residents. Less expensive and less intrusive methods of
crime deterrence should also be considered; public video surveillance is a tool, not a substitute for traditional law enforcement,
Gray declares. Gray is the mayor of Lancaster, Pennsylvania.*

As you read, consider the following questions:

1. What is the impact of security cameras on crime in
   Lancaster, in Gray's view?

2. As stated by the author, how can personnel be prevented
   from abusing security cameras?

J. Richard Gray, "Statement Re: Video Surveillance Camera Program," City of Lancaster,
PA, www.co.lancaster.pa.us, August 14, 2009. Reproduced by permission.

3. How does the author respond to the concern that video cameras can be used to follow law-abiding citizens?

First, let me be clear: I support the use of video cameras as an important tool that law enforcement and residents can rely upon to enhance public safety. While research has been inconclusive as to the impact of cameras on preventing crime, our own experience leaves no doubt that, but for the presence of video cameras, many perpetrators of both property crimes and violent crimes would not be apprehended and prosecuted. Crimes would not be solved and criminals would remain free to victimize our community. That said, I also acknowledge that concerns related to civil liberties and privacy rights are legitimate, and must be addressed whenever they arise, from whomever the source. The challenge we as a community and society face is how to use video surveillance technology to enhance our safety and apprehend criminals, while continuing to protect our civil liberties and the privacy that is so important to us.

We live in a world where technology is used to accumulate information about us on an almost daily basis. Our Internet accounts, credit cards, E-Z Passes, and cell phones all transmit, accumulate and store information about us. Our consumer preferences, travel patterns, and living habits all become known by those who are unknown to us. Cumulatively, this information can be misused to provide information about our private lives.

Video surveillance technology has also been growing exponentially in recent decades. Private monitoring now encompasses everything from a single camera in the neighborhood corner store, to multi-camera systems that are used to follow "suspicious" persons through shopping malls and parking lots. Security personnel and cameras monitor many of our public buildings. The lobby of the Lancaster City police station is monitored and the corridors of the Lancaster County Courthouse are monitored by Lancaster Deputy Sheriffs.

Born out of a 2001 Crime Commission recommendation, the Lancaster Community Safety Coalition's history and practice has consistently been driven by a commitment to the overall well being and safety of our community. There has been no hint of "big brotherism" or of any sinister plot to spy on others. Those that would make such allegations do so more for shock than substance. Working with residents, law enforcement, and in response to requests from community groups, the Lancaster Community Safety Coalition has used public and private funds to place cameras where they would be the most effective.

In the Lancaster Community Safety Coalition (LCSC) model there is no one building or parking lot being monitored. Rather, the Safety Coalition cameras are used to monitor public places, where people live, work, and play—places where irresponsible or targeted monitoring could do great damage to our sense of community and to our fundamental rights. . . .

Safeguards for Privacy

Some would argue that our constitutional rights to privacy and freedom from unreasonable search should be the ultimate standard by which to authorize the use of surveillance cameras. Constitutional safeguards represent a *minimum*, not a maximum definition of those rights. Therefore, the limits on government intrusion into an individual's privacy are not the only standards by which we should regulate video surveillance. In other words, just because you can constitutionally do it, doesn't mean that you should. For example, under certain circumstances the police can constitutionally look through your windows and into your home. I would certainly not agree that this should be allowed through the Safety Coalition's video surveillance, where we expect more than the minimal guarantees of privacy afforded by the Constitution.

Some have questioned the qualifications of those persons charged with monitoring Safety Coalition cameras. The LCSC Personnel Policies contain provisions for hiring and training of personnel. Prior to beginning work, background checks and drug testing is required. Once hired, drug testing can also be based on a "reasonable suspicion" or, on a random basis. All employees are required to sign a "Confidentiality Agreement" which prohibits discussion with "unauthorized persons" any events that are viewed. The Policies further limit the removal of materials including all "video records, CD's [sic], DVD's [sic], printed photographs, incident reports, Log Book data, monitoring methods, infrastructure plans, and all other materials . . ." The implementation and enforcement of these and other policies is important to earning the public trust necessary to operate such a program.

Also important, are the prohibitions contained in the Personnel Policies. There is a zero tolerance policy concerning the use of cameras for "personal gratification," or for "zooming of cameras deemed by the Executive Director to be unprofessional." Further, there is a specific prohibition against staff "engaging in racial profiling." Though both of these prohibitions are absolutely necessary, I have asked the Administration's representatives on the Board to further define specific standards for implementing the intent of these Policies, and to ensure that a system is in place to deal promptly and effectively with any policy violations that may occur.

The Safety Coalition has provided me with assurances that windows of buildings in the areas scanned by cameras are "masked" in such a way as to block any view into private properties. Understanding that the positioning of the cameras could allow views into properties not normally viewed from a street perspective, it is especially important that this rule be strictly enforced. Any evidence that Coalition cameras are used to view activities inside a building would be a violation of the public trust and, indeed, an affront to our right to pri-

Comfortable to Some

Indeed, in an age that empowers anyone with a cell phone camera and an Internet connection, we're all free to participate in this surge of information gathering and revelation. All of us can be spied on and engage in some high-visibility spying of our own.

"People have a desire to be protected," says Oscar Candy, professor emeritus at the University of Pennsylvania's Annenberg School for Communication. "We have this expectation that technology will solve the problem."

Jennifer King, a research specialist at the Samuelson Law, Technology & Public Policy Clinic at UC [University of California] Berkeley, believes that "surveillance feels comfortable to some people."

"There's a sense of guardianship, a feeling that someone is watching over me. It counteracts that aura of anonymity in the public space," she says.

Steven Winn,
San Francisco Chronicle,
August 21, 2007.

vacy. I can say without hesitation that I would be unwilling to support the use of cameras in public places unless strict measures are applied to protect the privacy of those inside buildings. A "reasonable expectation of privacy" should not require one to pull the blinds of every window of their home. Pursuant to this, I have directed the City's representatives on the Safety Coalition Board to provide assurances that such "masking" is in place, and to monitor the on-going use of "masking" so as to guarantee that privacy is maintained in our residents' buildings.

Advances, Uses, and Abuses

With continued advances in surveillance technology, important policy issues must be addressed: first, the use of facial recognition programs, and, second, the ability to "follow" a person from camera to camera, though that person is not currently engaged in criminal or suspicious activity. Both issues have as their distinguishing feature the deviation from "general surveillance" to specific focus of the cameras on an individual. Though neither of these practices, to my knowledge, is currently used by the LCSC, the advancement of technology and the expansion of the camera system compel us to address these issues.

While implicit public consent may have been given to random video surveillance, we should not assume that such consent has also been given for the employment of facial recognition technology that allows for tracking the movements of specific individuals. I have asked the City's Directors on the LCSC Board to examine this process and, prior to consent to implementation, have a full and open public discussion of the use of facial identification software; deciding if we want it at all and if so under what circumstances and with whose authorization.

With the expansion of the Safety Coalition camera system, we will soon have in excess of 160 cameras located throughout our City. This provides camera monitors with far greater capacity to follow a specific individual from location to location. My understanding of the current policy is that if a crime is being committed or "suspicious activity" is taking place, an individual involved may be followed from one location to another. This is understandable and reasonable. On the other hand, following someone from camera to camera while the person is neither breaking the law nor engaged in suspicious activity is a practice that could lend itself to serious abuse. Some would argue that if the police could do this, why not the cameras? Certainly, a commanding officer would not direct an officer to "tail" someone without some reason to believe that criminal activity was afoot. So too, with the use of cameras, the Police Bureau should be involved and documentation be made of each authorization to track an individual engaging in suspicious activity. I leave this to the LCSC Board to develop appropriate guidelines and agree that if requested the Lancaster City Bureau of Police will cooperate with internal policies.

Involving Residents in the Process

Special circumstances can arise where the mere presence of a camera could have a chilling effect on the performance of a legitimate objective. It has often been said, "If you have nothing to hide, why would you object to a camera?" As a general statement this may be correct. However, in the course of everyday life, we all engage in behaviors, though not criminal, that we would prefer remain private. Some obvious examples would be attendance at an infertility clinic, drug treatment program or an AA [Alcoholics Anonymous] meeting. Though none of these are illegal, they are certainly no one's business. A legitimate question is, would a camera in the vicinity of such a facility discourage those who might otherwise use the service? There should be a procedure to allow those with such concerns to formally bring it to the attention of the LCSC and, if found warranted, appropriate steps taken to address those concerns. These steps could range from "masking" a building or block, to removal of the camera or some other measure fashioned for the specific problem. There must be a process for evaluating and addressing such complaints either publicly or, if requested, privately. Again, I have directed the City's representatives to bring this issue before the Safety Coalition Board for full consideration.

A final future and present concern is of neighbors who simply elect not to have this type of surveillance in their neighborhood. Though my interaction with residents has generally involved requests for more cameras, some might wish not to have them at all. One solution might be to use the neighborhood Permitted Parking program model. This program requires that, first, a percentage of residents must request permitted parking; and then, a hearing is conducted to allow all sides to be aired. Perhaps a similar method could be employed to have a camera removed from a neighborhood if a sizable number of the residents so desire. Finally, formalized procedures must be established for more public notice of the future placement of cameras to allow the opportunity for dialogue with residents. Again, I have directed our representatives to bring this issue to the Board of Directors. . . .

Not a Silver Bullet

Finally, we must continue to evaluate the effectiveness of this system as compared to other less expensive and less intrusive forms of crime prevention. Though the camera system has provided a tool for law enforcement to solve crimes, it does not take the place of traditional law enforcement. The continued funding of such a system will be expensive, and with the City's dollars already stretched thin, the LCSC cannot rely on City taxpayers to fund future operating expenses. The LCSC must develop a sustainable plan for such funding. . . .

As we discuss surveillance cameras and the best way to use them, we would do well to remember that less expensive and less intrusive methods such as better neighborhood lighting or streetscapes that draw more people to our sidewalks are also effective "crime fighting" tools. Cameras are not a "silver bullet" solution to crime. Rather, we must continue to employ a multifaceted approach that will best serve our community. Cameras, when properly used and monitored, can be one of many weapons in our arsenal against crime.

| "It is impossible to tell what types of surveillance technologies the future will bring, but there are already examples of technologies that may run into challenges under the Fourth Amendment."

Public Video Surveillance Can Violate Privacy

Glen W. Fewkes

Glen W. Fewkes warns in the following viewpoint that the improvements in public video surveillance may pose new dangers to privacy and challenges for the courts. For example, backscatter X-ray technology in public would enable objects underneath a person's clothing to be viewed, and heart-sensing radar can determine a passerby's heart rate and respiration patterns from afar, Fewkes states. Thus, the author asserts, the reasonable expectation of privacy will become more legally complicated, and cities must use security cameras and developing systems within constitutional limits. Fewkes is a corporate attorney at Fox Rothschild in Philadelphia, Pennsylvania.

Glen W. Fewkes, "How Far Can Public Video Surveillance Go?" *Security Technology Executive*, October 2009, p. 40. Copyright 2009 Cygnus Business Media. All rights reserved. Reproduced by permission.

As you read, consider the following questions:

1. As stated by the author, a reasonable expectation of privacy rests on what two questions?

2. What did *Katz v. United States* establish, according to the author?

3. What constitutional challenge does heart-sensing radar technology raise, in the author's view?

By all accounts, 2008 was a boom year for the large-scale wireless video surveillance industry. "This is a modern version of the California gold rush, except that people are bringing cameras instead of pickaxes and shovels," says Stan Schatt, vice president of ABI Research.

Wireless video technology has allowed cities large and small to adopt high-tech video surveillance systems to enhance public safety, deter crime and act as a force multiplier for local law enforcement. Some research suggests that 75 percent of cities with active or planned wireless networks are either already running or planning to implement public safety applications. With public opinion increasingly tilting in favor of video surveillance systems, we can only expect to see larger and more advanced systems in the future.

For decades, cities have used basic video surveillance systems in public areas with little fear that they would run afoul of the Fourth Amendment prohibition against unreasonable searches and seizures. Long-standing Supreme Court decisions held that there is no reasonable expectation of privacy in things and actions in public view. As video surveillance technology continues to improve and merge with other surveillance technologies, however, older Court standards regarding the Fourth Amendment may prove less and less applicable. Cities currently operating or considering public video surveillance systems may be tempted to employ exciting new surveillance technologies, but they should proceed with caution as Fourth Amendment challenges may be just around the corner.

Fourth Amendment Basics

The Fourth Amendment of the United States Constitution protects the "right of the people to be secure in their persons, houses, papers and effects, against unreasonable searches and seizures." Government activities that qualify as a "search" must be accompanied by a properly issued warrant based on probable cause. If government video surveillance is not a "search" under the Fourth Amendment, then no warrant is required.

The United States Supreme Court has defined "search" broadly, such that even non-invasive surveillance may qualify. A "search" is not just a "physical intrusion into [a] given enclosure," but rather whenever a reasonable expectation of privacy is infringed. Whether an individual can claim a reasonable expectation of privacy rests on two questions: (1) has the individual shown that "he seeks to preserve [something] as private?" and (2) is the individual's subjective expectation of privacy "one that society is prepared to recognize as 'reasonable'?"

While infringement of a reasonable expectation of privacy is decided on a case-by-case basis, courts are especially likely to base their decisions on whether the surveilled things or actions were held out to public view in any way and on the level of intrusiveness of the surveillance technology.

Video Surveillance of Things in Public View. Courts have routinely held that individuals have no reasonable expectation of privacy to things or actions held out to public view, regardless of the individual's location. The Supreme Court has stated that "what a person knowingly exposes to the public, even in his home or office, is not a subject of Fourth Amendment protection." This includes the actions of a person on a public street, things inside a home that are still viewable through an open door or window, and even things on private property that the property owner has taken some measures to conceal but that are still viewable from a lawful vantage point.

In *California v. Ciraolo*, the Court determined that non-enhanced aerial photography of marijuana plants on Ciraolo's private property did not violate the Fourth Amendment, even though he had built 10-foot-high fences to prevent passersby from viewing his property. Visibility from any conceivable angle, including the airspace above, puts an object in public view. The Court stated: "The Fourth Amendment protection of the home has never been extended to require law enforcement officers to shield their eyes when passing by a home on public thoroughfares. Nor does the mere fact that an individual has taken measures to restrict some views of his activities preclude an officer's observations from a public vantage point where he has a right to be and which renders the activities clearly visible." Simply put, if it is visible with the naked eye from a public vantage point, then it is not protected by the Fourth Amendment.

Using Enhancing Technology in the Surveillance of Public Areas. No court has found enhanced video surveillance of a public area to be a search under the Fourth Amendment, but dicta by the Supreme Court leave open the possibility.

Despite the general rule that there is no reasonable expectation of privacy to things or actions held out to public view, the Court has clearly stated that "people are not shorn of all Fourth Amendment protection when they step from their homes onto the public sidewalks." *Katz v. United States* established that under the right circumstances, an individual may be able to claim a reasonable expectation of privacy even when in a public area. In *Katz*, the Court found that warrantless interception of a conversation in a public telephone booth violated the Fourth Amendment. Katz had manifested an intent to keep his conversation private by entering the phone booth and closing the door, and the Court determined that privacy within a public phone booth was something that society was prepared to accept as reasonable.

The Supreme Court has also recognized the possibility that surveillance with enhancing technology, when used in public areas, might infringe on a reasonable expectation of privacy. In *United States v. Knotts*, police officers used a beeper tracking device planted in a car to monitor the car's movements. While "nothing in the Fourth Amendment prohibited the police from augmenting the sensory faculties bestowed upon them at birth with such enhancement as science and technology afforded them," the Court's decision rested on the fact that the enhancing technology (the beeper tracking device) was simply a "more effective means of observing what is already public." The Court's implication is that technology that allows the observation of things that are not in public view may run afoul of the Fourth Amendment. Similarly, in *Dow Chemical Co. v. United States*, the Court noted that certain levels of surveillance detail, such as zooming in on a finger to identify a class ring, may violate the Fourth Amendment, even in a non-home environment.

If it is possible for surveillance technology in public areas to violate the Fourth Amendment, how will we know when it does? What will that technology look like and how will the Supreme Court analyze the technology's use? Only time will tell the answers to some of these questions, but based on the Supreme Court's standard for privacy, the offending technology would need to be capable of observing something that an individual has sought to protect as private in a way that society is prepared to recognize as reasonable. The Supreme Court may determine that when a technology makes visible those things that would not otherwise be visible without physical intrusion, it may violate the Fourth Amendment. Still, this question would be decided on the facts of each case, and "not by extravagant generalizations" or merely the technology's potential to invade privacy.

Troublesome Technologies on the Horizon

It is impossible to tell what types of surveillance technologies the future will bring, but there are already examples of technologies that may run into challenges under the Fourth Amendment. Included here are just two examples:

Backscatter X-Ray. Backscatter X-ray technology uses a narrow, low intensity X-ray beam scanned over the surface of a body or other object at high speed. The result is a detailed picture of the scanned individual's body, displaying all items that the individual may be carrying on his/her person, even under clothing, or displaying the contents of the scanned object. The American Civil Liberties Union has referred to the technology as a "virtual strip search." Backscatter X-ray technology is already in use at some airport security stations as an alternative to invasive pat-down searches, and at border terminals as a method of scanning the contents of cars and cargo containers.

The Fourth Amendment does not apply in the same manner in these high-security contexts, where there individuals have "consented" to such searches by virtue of choosing to fly in an airplane or crossing the border. As this technology develops, however, its migration to main street is becoming more apparent. The Z Backscatter Van from American Science and Engineering Inc. [AS&E], places a backscatter X-ray unit within an ordinary looking delivery van. The van can drive by cars and trucks to scan the contents of trunks and cargo holds, or, if parked by the side of a street, it can scan passing vehicles and pedestrians. AS&E is marketing the van as a tool for homeland security and "urban surveillance."

Pairing backscatter X-ray technology with a public video surveillance system would allow a view of individuals not only as they appear to the public on a street, but also of every item that the individual may be carrying under their clothing. Backscatter X-ray may be just the type of technology that the Court in *Knotts* pondered that goes beyond merely augmenting vision to seeing those things that are not otherwise visible to the public. If the area beneath an individual's clothes is one that society is prepared to recognize as private, which seems likely, then this may be a Fourth Amendment violation.

Heart Sensing Radar. On December 15, 2008, the Department of Homeland Security issued a Privacy Impact Assessment for the Future Attribute Screening Technology (FAST) Project. The FAST Project will test technology linking video surveillance with a remote sensor that can measure the heart rate and respiration patterns of a subject from a distance and without physical contact. The technology could be used to remotely identify the physiological status of an individual and help determine whether that individual may be about to commit a crime or cause a disturbance, based on, for example, a racing heart rate.

Heart Sensing Radar is already being marketed by private companies. On January 9, 2009, Kai Sensors Inc., issued a news release touting a recent partnership that will help bring the technology to market for use in "law enforcement missions" and "intelligence gathering." While no cities have disclosed using Heart Sensing Radar in connection with public video surveillance yet, the possibility is clearly in the foreseeable future.

Heart Sensing Radar technology gives a clear example of the types of questions Courts will be forced to consider in the near future with respect to the Fourth Amendment. Certainly an individual does not have a reasonable expectation of privacy as to their stressed or excited physical appearance, but what about as to the movements of their bodily organs hidden from public view? Such a question was unfathomable even a year ago.

The proliferation of public video surveillance systems and new surveillance technologies provide exciting potential in the world of public safety and law enforcement. However, new technologies also raise new legal questions. The longstanding

Supreme Court standard that individuals have no reasonable expectation of privacy to things held out to public view becomes more complicated as new surveillance equipment has the ability to see more and more. Cities may be wise to adopt public video surveillance systems, but they should proceed with caution to ensure that their systems do not have the potential to violate the Fourth Amendment.

> "The new e-passports [are] far more se-
> cure than today's documents."

Electronic Passports Protect Americans

Security

In the following viewpoint, Security *maintains that electronic passports protect travelers and international borders.* Security *states that since 2007, U.S. passports feature chips that contain a digital photograph of the owner and data from the information page. This deters counterfeiting and unauthorized passport use in two ways, writes* Security: *First, the printed information must be compared to digital information on the chip by passport control. Second, the chip is locked, which makes tampering or falsified data detectable.* Security *is a magazine that covers innovations and issues in the security industry.*

As you read, consider the following questions:

1. Why is copying data from an electronic passport useless, in Randy Vanderhoof's opinion?

2. What happens at points of entry with electronic passports, as stated in the viewpoint?

Security, "ePassport, eSecurity, eehPrivacy," September 2006, pp. 14, 20, 22. Copyright © 2006 BNP Media. Reproduced by permission.

3. According to *Security*, how is the digital information in an electronic passport kept private?

For identification technology, whether public or private, the goal has been verification of identity at the cost of some convenience. But what about privacy and real security?

Not so suddenly, enterprises and their chief security officers must balance increased security with concerns centering on privacy and hacker intrusions.

A case in point: Gemalto [a digital security company] last month [August 2006] receives an order for the U.S. Electronic Passport when the United States Government Printing Office (GPO) placed its first order with the company, following Gemalto's electronic passport technology qualification completion. The GPO and U.S. Department of State evaluated the solution at their testing Facilities and confirmed it fully satisfies the agency's requirements for privacy protection, security, durability, manufacturing yield, and transaction speed and communications performance. The GPO, on behalf of the U.S. Department of State, plans to incorporate the electronic capability in all new passports to be issued in 2007. The United States produced over ten million passports in 2005.

The electronic passport (e-passport) technology includes a secure operating system software running in a large capacity contactless microprocessor chip. The chip is embedded in a module that is highly resistant to damage and then is integrated into the passport booklet cover.

Sensitive Chip Information

The computer chip in the passport will contain all the information that is now printed on the document's data page including a digitized photograph of the passport owner. The text data and the photograph can be read with a contactless reader at a border entry point and the electronically provided data can be compared to the information printed in the passport at issuance.

Not to be confused with RFID [radio frequency identification], secure personal identification devices using contactless smart card technology have built-in and active security and encryption capabilities to protect information access and communications. More than 30 nations worldwide have already pledged to adopt passport technology that conforms to an international standard for electronic identification data. Some have raised security concerns.

A recent security conference hosted by Black Hat suggests that biometric e-passports used in the UK [United Kingdom] and other countries can be hacked. The demonstration exposed a vulnerability that could potentially allow criminals to clone embedded code and enter countries illegally.

Luke Grunwald, a security consultant with DN-Systems in Germany, demonstrated how data stored in the passport could be transferred onto bank chips, which could be implanted in forged passports.

But according to Randy Vanderhoof, executive director of the Smart Card Alliance, "The smart card industry does not see a security threat for electronic passports when data can be copied because the data can't be changed or altered. Even if someone could copy the information on your chip, it doesn't achieve anything, because that information is locked. It can't be changed."

Enhanced Security Measures

"It's of no use to anyone else because your picture is on the chip and they're not you. It's no different than someone trying to use a lost or stolen passport. The whole program is designed to eliminate the risks of anyone altering or using someone else's passport credential, and it does."

The objectives of this global program were to make passports virtually impossible to counterfeit and prevent anyone other than the passport owner from using it. The e-passport program achieves that in two ways:

- First, the information on the printed page, including the bearer's photograph, is stored on the chip and displayed on a screen at passport control. By comparing the digital information, the printed passport and the person, passport control can confirm everything is OK. They will immediately see a discrepancy if someone is attempting to use someone else's chip information.

- Second, the information on the chip is digitally signed by the issuing country's passport authority. That information is locked and any changes would be detected at passport control. It also means any attempt to create false data and a fake passport credential would be detected. Unlike today's paper passport, where a photo can potentially be replaced, the digital photo and other information on the e-passport chip cannot be changed.

Together these two capabilities mean that no one could use a lost or stolen passport, or even a copy of one, to illegally enter the country. This makes the new e-passports far more secure than today's documents. Other features prevent anyone from reading U.S. e-passports without the holder handing it over and the cover opened. This protects people's privacy.

Conflict with Existing Technology

Beyond e-passports, there continues to be legislative fights over radio frequency identification systems.

A number of proposals in California introduced by State Senator Joe Simitian, has grabbed the attention of the security industry. In a letter to the Senator recently, the executive director of the Security Industry Association, Richard Chace, said that the Security Industry Association (SIA) respectfully expresses its opposition to Senate Bill 768, the Identity Information Protection Act of 2005, and related legislation (Senate Bills 432, 682, and 1078) that could severely impede the use of Radio Frequency Identification (RFID) technology. SIA is an international trade association and leading voice for more than 340 manufacturers, distributors, and integrators of electronic and physical security equipment.

SIA and its members agree there may be some legitimate concerns about the use of RFID technology in certain applications. However, we strongly believe these legislative proposals could have dire unintended consequences on technology used to ensure the validity of identification credentials. The legislation could set several dangerous precedents: The legislation seems to assume that technology innovation is static; in reality, problems are addressed quickly through the rapid technological evolution for which our industry is known. SIA is concerned that your legislation could lock in a set of criteria that will be obsolete and actually less safe than what technology could make available tomorrow.

In our opinion, the aforementioned Senate bills give the appearance of favoring particular technologies by banning or restricting the use of RFID to very specific applications. This is neither a customary nor advisable purpose of legislative activity.

What Happens at Passport Control

1. The officer swipes the data page through a special reader to read the two lines of printed characters on the bottom of the data page. This provides a key that's unique to the passport and lets the process proceed.

2. The officer holds your open passport over another reader, then checks his view of you (a), with the photo in your passport (b), and all the data from your passport (including your photo) on the monitor (c).

3. The data on the monitor also verifies that your passport was issued by a legitimate authority, and that it has not been altered.

4. A chip is embedded into the back cover. It contains data that cannot be read without the security key as shown in step one above.

5. When the passport is held over the reader (no contact is necessary), a radio field from the reader wakes up the chip, and the encrypted data is transferred to the reader, allowing the officer to conduct his visual check.

6. A thin radio shield can be sandwiched between the front cover and the first page. Whenever the passport is closed—for instance, in your pocket or briefcase—the digital information in the chip cannot be read. The shield will not set off airport metal detectors.

"The chips could be skimmed from a yard away ... all a hacker would need to read e-passport numbers, say, in an elevator."

Electronic Passports Threaten Privacy

Todd Lewan

In the following viewpoint, Todd Lewan contends that electronic passports are vulnerable to identity theft and interception. Lewan claims that their tag numbers can be read from yards away and directly linked to the individuals. These privacy concerns are shared not only by the public, he states, but also by experts and federal officials. Furthermore, Lewan also alleges that if paired with facial recognition and other technologies, electronic passports may enable the government to secretly identify, monitor, and track citizens in real-time. The author is a former writer for the Associated Press.

As you read, consider the following questions:

1. What was hacker Chris Paget able to achieve in twenty minutes, as described by Lewan?

Todd Lewan, "As Government Tags Passports, Licenses, Critics Fear Privacy Is 'Chipped' Away," *San Francisco Examiner*, July 12, 2009. Copyright © 2010 The Associated Press. All rights reserved. Reprinted with permission of the Associated Press.

2. What did the Homeland Security's advisory committee report about radio-frequency identification (RFID) technology, as stated by Lewan?

3. Why does the potential to remotely copy RFID numbers from passports and other forms of ID worry experts, according to Lewan?

Climbing into his Volvo, outfitted with a Matrics antenna and a Motorola reader he'd bought on eBay for $190, Chris Paget cruised the streets of San Francisco with this objective: To read the identity cards of strangers, wirelessly, without ever leaving his car.

It took him 20 minutes to strike hacker's gold.

Zipping past Fisherman's Wharf, his scanner downloaded to his laptop the unique serial numbers of two pedestrians' electronic U.S. passport cards embedded with radio frequency identification, or RFID, tags. Within an hour, he'd "skimmed" four more of the new, microchipped PASS [passport] cards from a distance of 20 feet.

Little Brother

Increasingly, government officials are promoting the chipping of identity documents as a 21st-century application of technology that will help speed border crossings, safeguard credentials against counterfeiters, and keep terrorists from sneaking into the country.

But Paget's February [2009] experiment demonstrated something privacy advocates had feared for years: That RFID, coupled with other technologies, could make people trackable without their knowledge.

He filmed his heist, and soon his video went viral on the Web, intensifying a debate over a push by government, federal and state, to put tracking technologies in identity documents and over their potential to erode privacy.

Putting a traceable RFID in every pocket has the potential to make everybody a blip on someone's radar screen, critics say, and to redefine Orwellian [referring to novelist George Orwell's depiction of civil injustices] government snooping for the digital age.

"Little Brother," some are already calling it [reflecting Orwell's concept of "Big Brother"]—even though elements of the global surveillance web they warn against exist only on drawing boards, neither available nor approved for use.

But with advances in tracking technologies coming at an ever-faster rate, critics say, it won't be long before governments could be able to identify and track anyone in real time, 24-7, from a cafe in Paris to the shores of California.

On June 1, [2009,] it became mandatory for Americans entering the United States by land or sea from Canada, Mexico, Bermuda and the Caribbean to present identity documents embedded with RFID tags, though conventional passports remain valid until they expire.

Among new options are the chipped "e-passport," and the new, electronic PASS card—credit-card sized, with the bearer's digital photograph and a chip that can be scanned through a pocket, backpack or purse from 30 feet.

Alternatively, travelers can use "enhanced" driver's licenses embedded with RFID tags now being issued in some border states: Washington, Vermont, Michigan and New York. Texas and Arizona have entered into agreements with the federal government to offer chipped licenses, and the U.S. Department of Homeland Security [DHS] has recommended expansion to non-border states. Kansas and Florida officials have received DHS briefings on the licenses, agency records show.

The purpose of using RFID is not to identify people, says Mary Ellen Callahan, the chief privacy officer at Homeland Security, but "to verify that the identification document holds valid information about you."

An RFID document that doubles as a U.S. travel credential "only makes it easier to pull the right record fast enough, to make sure that the border flows, and is operational"—even though a 2005 Government Accountability Office report found that government RFID readers often failed to detect travelers' tags.

A Fundamental Flaw

Critics warn that RFID-tagged identities will enable identity thieves and other criminals to commit "contactless" crimes against victims who won't immediately know they've been violated.

Neville Pattinson, vice president for government affairs at Gemalto, Inc., a major supplier of microchipped cards, is no RFID basher. He's a board member of the Smart Card Alliance, an RFID industry group, and is serving on the Department of Homeland Security's Data Privacy and Integrity Advisory Committee.

In a 2007 article published by a newsletter for privacy professionals, Pattinson called the chipped cards vulnerable "to attacks from hackers, identity thieves and possibly even terrorists."

RFID, he wrote, has a fundamental flaw: Each chip is built to faithfully transmit its unique identifier "in the clear, exposing the tag number to interception during the wireless communication."

Once a tag number is intercepted, "it is relatively easy to directly associate it with an individual," he says. "If this is done, then it is possible to make an entire set of movements posing as somebody else without that person's knowledge."

Echoing these concerns were the AeA—the lobbying association for technology firms—the Smart Card Alliance, the Institute of Electrical and Electronics Engineers, the Business Travel Coalition, and the Association of Corporate Travel Executives.

Meanwhile, Homeland Security has been promoting broad use of RFID even though its own advisory committee on data integrity and privacy issued caveats. In its 2006 draft report, the committee concluded that RFID "increases risks to personal privacy and security, with no commensurate benefit for performance or national security," and recommended that "RFID be disfavored for identifying and tracking human beings."

For now, chipped PASS cards and enhanced driver's licenses [EDLs] are not yet widely deployed in the United States. To date, roughly 192,000 EDLs have been issued in Washington, Vermont, Michigan and New York.

But as more Americans carry them "you can bet that long-range tracking of people on a large scale will rise exponentially," says Paget, a self-described "ethical hacker" who works as an Internet security consultant.

But Gigi Zenk, a spokeswoman for the Washington state Department of Licensing, says Americans "aren't that concerned about the RFID" in a time when "tracking an individual is much easier through a cell phone."

American Citizens Have Grave Concerns

In the wake of the September 11 [2001, terrorist] attacks—and the finding that some terrorists entered the United States using phony passports—the State Department proposed mandating that Americans and foreign visitors carry "enhanced" passport booklets, with microchips embedded in the covers.

In February 2005, when the State Department asked for public comment, it got an outcry: Of the 2,335 comments received, 98.5 percent were negative, with 86 percent expressing security or privacy concerns, the department reported in an October 2005 notice in the *Federal Register*.

Identity theft and "fears that the U.S. Government or other governments would use the chip to track and censor, intimidate or otherwise control or harm them" were of "grave concern," it noted. Many Americans worried "that the information could be read at distances in excess of 10 feet."

Those citizens, it turns out, had cause.

According to department records obtained by researchers at the University of California, Berkeley, under a Freedom of Information Act [FOIA] request and reviewed by the AP [Associated Press], discussion about security concerns with the e-passport occurred as early as January 2003 but tests weren't ordered until the department began receiving public criticism two years later.

When the AP asked when testing was initiated, the State Department said only that "a battery of durability and electromagnetic tests were performed" by the National Institute of Standards and Technology, along with tests "to measure the ability of data on electronic passports to be surreptitiously skimmed or for communications with the chip reader to be eavesdropped," testing which "led to additional privacy controls being placed on U.S. electronic passports. . . ."

In 2005, the department incorporated metallic fibers into the e-passport's front cover, to reduce the read range, and added encryptions and a feature that required inspectors to optically scan the e-passport first for the chip to communicate wirelessly.

New Passport Chips Make for Easy Reading

But what of concerns about the e-passport's read range?

In its October 2005 *Federal Register* notice, the State Department reassured Americans that the e-passport's chip would emit radio waves only within a 4-inch radius, making it tougher to hack.

But in May 2006, at the University of Tel Aviv, researchers directly skimmed an encrypted tag from several feet away. At the University of Cambridge in Britain, a student intercepted a transmission between an e-passport and a legitimate reader from 160 feet.

Corrupt Data and Malicious Codes

In addition to the danger of counterfeiting, [security consultant Lukas] Grunwald says that the ability to tamper with e-passports opens up the possibility that someone could write corrupt data to the passport RFID [radio frequency identification] tag that would crash an unprepared inspection system, or even introduce malicious code into the backend border-screening computers. This would work, however, only if the backend system suffers from the kind of built-in software vulnerabilities that have made other systems so receptive to viruses and Trojan-horse attacks.

"I want to say to people that if you're using RFID passports, then please make it secure," Grunwald says. "This is in your own interest and it's also in my interest. If you think about cyberterrorists and nasty, black-hat type of guys, it's a high risk. . . . From my point of view, it should not be possible to clone the passport at all."

Kim Zetter, Wired, *August 2006.*

The State Department, according to its own records obtained under FOIA, was aware of the problem months before its *Federal Register* notice and more than a year before the e-passport was rolled out in August 2006.

"Do not claim that these chips can only be read at a distance of 10 cm (4 inches)," Frank Moss, deputy assistant Secretary of State for passport services, wrote in an April 22, 2005, e-mail to Randy Vanderhoof, executive director of the Smart Card Alliance. "That really has been proven to be wrong."

The chips could be skimmed from a yard away, he added—all a hacker would need to read e-passport numbers, say, in an elevator.

In February 2006, an encrypted Dutch e-passport was hacked on national television, and later, British e-passports were hacked. The State Department countered that European e-passports weren't as safe as their American counterparts because they lacked safety features such as the anti-skimming cover. Recent studies have shown, however, that more powerful readers can penetrate that metal sheathing.

The RFIDs in enhanced driver's licenses and PASS cards contain a silicon computer chip attached to a wire antenna, which transmits a unique identifier via radio waves when "awakened" by an electromagnetic reader.

The technology they use is designed to track products through the supply chain. These chips, known as EPCglobal Gen 2, are intended to release their data to any inquiring Gen 2 reader within a 30-foot radius.

Hacking and Tracking

The government says remotely readable ID cards transmit only RFID numbers, which correspond to records stored in secure government databases. Even if a hacker were to copy an RFID number onto a blank tag and place it into a counterfeit ID, officials say, the forger's face still wouldn't match the true cardholder's photo in the database.

Still, computer experts say government databases can be hacked. Others worry about a day when hackers might deploy readers at "chokepoints," such as checkout lines, skim RFID numbers from people's driver's licenses, then pair those numbers to personal data skimmed from chipped credit cards (though credit cards are harder to skim). They imagine stalkers skimming RFID tags to track their targets, and fear government agents compiling chip numbers at peace rallies, mosques or gun shows, simply by strolling through a crowd with a reader.

Others worry more about the linking of chips with other identification methods, including biometric technologies, such as facial recognition.

Should biometrics be coupled with RFID, "governments will have, for the first time in history, the means to identify, monitor and track citizens anywhere in the world in real time," says Mark Lerner, spokesman for the Constitutional Alliance, a network of nonprofit groups, lawmakers and citizens opposed to remotely readable identity and travel documents.

The International Civil Aviation Organization, the U.N. agency that sets global standards for passports, now calls for facial recognition in all e-passports.

Periodical Bibliography

The following articles have been selected to supplement the diverse views presented in this chapter.

Steve Boggan	"'Fakeproof' e-Passport Is Cloned in Minutes," *Times Online* (London), August 6, 2008. www.timesonline.co.uk.
Andrew Brown	"They Know All About You," *Guardian* (Manchester, UK), August 28, 2006. www.guardian.co.uk.
Leslie Harris	"The Power of All," *Huffington Post*, December 3, 2009. www.huffingtonpost.com.
Linda Hass	"Internet Use Requires Responsibility," *Jackson (MI) Citizen Patriot*, October 10, 2009. www.citpat.com.
Rose Lombardi	"Privacy Matters in Public Surveillance," *Canadian Security*, December 2007.
Ron Panko	"Caught on Video," *Best's Review*, August 2009.
William Petroski	"Cameras Enter All Corners of Life," *Des Moines Register*, December 6, 2009.
Mattathias Schwartz	"The Trolls Among Us," *New York Times*, August 3, 2008.
David Talbot	"Dissent Made Safer," *Technology Review*, May/June 2009.
Matt Villano	"Does the Eye Spy?" *T.H.E. Journal*, November 2007.

CHAPTER 3

Is Medical Privacy Adequately Protected?

Chapter Preface

In the United States, most companies, businesses, and organizations are not required to test employees for drug use. The federal and state governments also have laws that restrict drug testing except for certain occupations. Employers in the private sector, however, have the right to screen employees for substance abuse. They do not have to follow the regulations established by the Substance Abuse and Mental Health Services Administration (SAMHSA), but that is recommended in order to stay within legal bounds. About 55 million drug tests are conducted in the American workplace each year.

Proponents of drug testing assert that an employee's dependence problems hurt the entire organization, from lowered productivity, to abuse of sick leave, to draining of resources. Compared with nonusers, drug users are absent 50 percent more, use nearly double the employment benefits, and file more than twice the workers' compensation claims, according to SAMHSA. William F. Current, an author and expert on substance abuse in the workplace, strongly advises preemployment drug screening. "As employers avoid hiring drug users, they save thousands of dollars each year through reduced accidents, absenteeism, theft, violence, and health care costs."[1]

Nonetheless, opponents of drug testing maintain that it can reveal health information that is sensitive and may lead to discrimination against workers and job candidates. Writer Dave Olson alleges that screening can reveal pregnancy, the use of legal prescription drugs such as antidepressants, and genetic conditions and makeup. Such information can also spread through indiscretion, he warns: "Besides the observation is the handling of test results which may pass through many hands, including hospital and lab staff, compromising

1. William F. Current, "Cut Costs and Increase Safety with Pre-employment Drug Testing," *EHS Today*, July 23, 2002. http://ehstoday.com/mag/ehs_imp_35676/.

integrity and confidentiality especially in a small community. Further, results or rumors may be inappropriately distributed amongst company or industry causing damage to professional and personal reputation."[2] In the following chapter, the authors weigh in on the issues concerning medical privacy.

2. Dave Olson, "Privacy Issues in Workplace Drug Testing," Spring 2004. http://uncleweed.net/words/essays/Workplace-Drug-Testing.pdf.

> *"By collecting DNA from arrestees, law enforcement can identify criminals earlier and create more efficient investigation practices."*

Law Enforcement DNA Databanks Can Protect Americans

DNA Saves

In the following viewpoint, DNA Saves promotes the nationwide legalization of DNA testing of arrestees charged with felony crimes. The organization declares that DNA records are the most powerful tool in forensic investigations, and DNA databanks are crucial in solving violent crimes, capturing criminals, and exonerating the innocent. Medical privacy would not be threatened, states DNA Saves, as law enforcement have no use for collecting genetic indicators or health information. The organization was formed in New Mexico by Dave and Jayann Sepich in 2008. The Sepichs worked in their state to pass "Katie's Law," which is named after their daughter who was murdered in 2003.

DNA Saves, "What Is DNA Testing?" and "Why Pass Law?" dnasaves.org. Accessed January 4, 2010. Reproduced by permission.

As you read, consider the following questions:

1. How does DNA Saves describe the steps of DNA collecting and analyzing?

2. Why is forensic analysis of DNA not a privacy concern, in the view of DNA Saves?

3. What did the Chicago Study reveal, according to DNA Saves?

DNA is the most powerful tool available for identification in forensic investigations. Because of its ability to link physical evidence found at a crime scene to a single person, it is often referred to as a "digital fingerprint." This method is so precise that it can ensure pinpoint accuracy, down to one in a billion. And, unlike fingerprints, which can only be found if a suspect touches something, DNA exists in every cell of the human body, from hair and blood to skin and tears, and can be shed or deposited while committing a crime. That means it is often the only means for accurate identification.

DNA databases make it possible for law enforcement crime laboratories to electronically search and compare collected DNA profiles to crime scene evidence. In the United States, the Combined DNA Index System (CODIS) links all local, state, and national databases and contains more than 5 million records. Currently, legislation exists on the federal level and in 21 states, enabling investigators to collect DNA upon arrest for certain felony crimes.

The process for collecting and analyzing DNA is minimally invasive and only takes a few steps:

- Lightly swab the inside of an arrestee's cheek

- Analyze the sample to obtain a unique identifier containing only the 13 to 15 key markers required to confirm identity

- Enter the sample into the CODIS, where it can be compared against forensic evidence from crime scenes across the country

Not a Privacy Concern

While some have raised concerns about the privacy rights of persons accused of serious crimes, DNA testing of arrestees can actually protect civil liberties. Moreover, crime laboratories and investigators would have no need of such predictive health information as it is of no value in a criminal investigation. Through a forensic DNA profile, it is impossible to obtain medical information and genetic indicators. Forensic analysts only analyze the 13 to 15 key markers that make identification possible. And, unlike fingerprints, the DNA profile is stored in CODIS as a numeric file, with absolutely no access to personal information (not even the person's name) or criminal background. Crime scene evidence matching this profile will lead police to the right suspect, regardless of race or economic status, thereby reducing the incidence of racial profiling and other objectionable means of developing suspects.

Why Pass This Law?

States have been collecting DNA from convicted felons for almost two decades, and it's helped solve thousands of crimes. But, we can do more. By passing arrestee DNA legislation, law enforcement officials can catch criminals sooner, save more lives and use DNA to its full potential. Collected at the same time as fingerprints, DNA testing only requires a simple cheek swab upon arrest. That's why Congress and a few pioneering states have already passed laws for DNA Arrestee Testing.

Arrestee testing will help your state to:

- Catch repeat offenders sooner

- Prevent violent crimes

- Exonerate the innocent

- Protect civil liberties

- Reduce criminal justice costs

The Facts:

- Since 1974, more than 90 percent of all state prisoners have been repeat offenders

- 70% of America's crime is committed by 6% of its criminals

- With DNA arrestee testing on the books since 2003, Virginia has received over 5,000 hits on their database, with nearly 500 of these matches directly attributable to arrestees

- 1 out of every 6 American women have been the victims of an attempted or completed rape

- To date, post-conviction DNA testing has led to the exoneration of more than 200 wrongfully convicted individuals in the United States, and many of these individuals were not fully exonerated until after a DNA match was made on the database to another offender

- 21 States have enacted legislation to require DNA from certain felony arrestees, and even more states are considering such laws

The Chicago Study

In 2005, the City of Chicago demonstrated the prevalence of repeat crime and the importance of arrestee testing. By taking a closer look at the criminal history of eight convicted felons, the Chicago Study uncovered startling results—60 violent crimes could have been prevented if only DNA had been collected for a prior felony arrest. In each case, the offender had committed previously undetected violent crimes that investigators could have identified immediately through a DNA match.

Unfortunately, DNA was not required at arrest. The eight offenders in Chicago accumulated a total of 21 felony arrests before law enforcement officials were finally able to convict them of violent crimes.

With DNA arrestee testing, the following crimes could have been prevented:

- 22 murders—victims ranging from 24 to 44 years of age

- 30 rapes—victims ranging from 15 to 65 years of age

- Attempted rapes

- Aggravated kidnapping

- Protecting civil liberties

Privacy Rights Intact

While often challenged on Constitutional grounds, courts throughout the country have overwhelmingly upheld DNA database statutes. These decisions and the supporting rationale have been clear that the processes, procedures, and benefits of collecting DNA from those arrested for serious crimes is as constitutionally sound as the collection of fingerprints.

The Fourth Amendment to the US Constitution protects individuals from searches and seizures which are "unreasonable." For years, the Courts, including the US Supreme Court, have found that, when a suspect is arrested with probable cause, his identification becomes a matter of legitimate state interest. The rationale behind the decision is the fact that the identification of suspects is "relevant not only to solving the crime for which the suspect is arrested, but also for maintaining a permanent record to solve other past and future crimes." This becomes particularly clear when we consider the universal nature of "booking" procedures that are followed for every suspect arrested for a felony, whether or not the proof of a particular suspect's crime will involve fingerprint evidence or an eyewitness identification for which mug shots could be used.

Treating the taking of DNA samples at arrest just like fingerprinting at arrest has been widely accepted. Consider these additional examples:

- The Second Circuit [Court] held "[t]he collection and maintenance of DNA information, while effected through relatively more intrusive procedures such as blood draws or buccal cheek swabs, in our view plays the same role as fingerprinting."

- The Third Circuit held "[t]he governmental justification for [DNA] identification relies on no argument different in kind from that traditionally advanced for taking fingerprints and photographs, but with additional force because of the potentially greater precision of DNA sampling and matching methods."

- The Ninth Circuit held "[t]hat the gathering of DNA information requires the drawing of blood rather than inking and rolling a person's fingertips does not elevate the intrusion upon the plaintiffs' Fourth Amendment interests to a level beyond minimal."

- The State of Maryland held "The purpose [of the DNA profile] is akin to that of a fingerprint."

- New Jersey held, "We harbor no doubt that the taking of a buccal cheek swab is a very minor physical intrusion upon the person. . . . [T]hat intrusion is no more intrusive than the fingerprint procedure and the taking of one's photograph that a person must already undergo as part of the normal arrest process."

Protecting the Innocent and Missing

While we fully recognize the concerns that have been raised about personal privacy, we cannot overstate the critical and increased role that DNA is playing in our system of justice. Not only is it used to identify those who commit crimes, but equally if not more important it can play the determining role in exonerating the innocent. People who are now being exonerated of crimes would never have been arrested in the first place had today's DNA technology been in place. It has even been suggested that greater use of DNA technology is in order to help to identify missing persons and to protect those who may some day go missing.

State of Connecticut, Division of Criminal Justice,
March 20, 2008.

- Oregon held, "Because using a swab to take a DNA sample from the mucous membrane of an arrestee's cheek is akin to the fingerprinting of a person in custody, we conclude that the seizure of defendant's DNA did not constitute an unreasonable seizure under the constitution."

- The Virginia State Supreme Court held "the taking of [the suspect's] DNA sample upon arrest in Stafford County pursuant to Code § 19.2-310.2:1 is analogous to the taking of a suspect's fingerprints upon arrest and was not an unlawful search under the Fourth Amendment."

Reducing Costs

By collecting DNA from arrestees, law enforcement can identify criminals earlier and create more efficient investigation practices. Solving crimes sooner reduces costs associated with misdirected investigations. With a DNA match, law enforcement can quickly narrow in on the right suspect, saving untold manhours and manpower used in traditional investigations. This cost savings can then be redirected to other crimes where DNA is not available and traditional investigation techniques are the only means of solving the crime. With a DNA match, persons wrongfully accused of committing a crime can be freed sooner. Consider the case of Robert Gonzalez who provided a false confession and was in danger of a wrongful conviction until a match was made on the DNA database—a match to a DNA sample collected under Katie's Law [a 2006 bill that requires DNA sampling in New Mexico, named for a crime victim] from a felony arrestee. With a DNA match, more crimes can be prevented, such as those in the Chicago Study, or the cases from California, Maryland, Texas, and Washington State. How do we put a price on the cost of saving a life or preventing a rape? What is the cost of knowing we could have done something to prevent these crimes, and chose not to?

│ *"Compelling persons to provide their*
│ *DNA to law enforcement agencies raises*
│ *concerns about . . . individual and fa-*
│ *milial privacy."*

Law Enforcement DNA Databanks Can Threaten Medical Privacy

Karen J. Maschke

In the following viewpoint, Karen J. Maschke argues that DNA databanks for law enforcement and criminal investigations can imperil privacy. Maschke claims that advances in technology will make it possible to determine an individual's ancestry, genetic conditions, and other personal medical information from forensic DNA profiles. Additionally, she posits that innocent people may be harassed to submit DNA samples and placed under "genetic surveillance" without probable cause. The use of DNA databanks for genetic research to determine criminality, says Maschke, is also a concern. Maschke is a research scholar at the Hastings Center and editor of IRB: Ethics & Human Research.

Karen J. Maschke, *From Birth to Death and Bench to Clinic: The Hastings Center Bioethics Briefing Book for Journalists, Policymakers, and Campaigns*, Garrison, NY: Hastings Center, 2008. Copyright © 2008, The Hastings Center. All rights reserved. Reproduced by permission.

As you read, consider the following questions:

1. How did state lawmakers expand the categories of groups required to submit DNA in 2007, as told by the author?

2. In the author's view, how are the procedures changing for the release of identifying information based on partial DNA matches?

3. What are "backdoor" methods of obtaining DNA, as described by the author?

The European Court of Human Rights in Strasbourg [France] is expected to decide in 2008 whether the United Kingdom can permanently keep the DNA samples and profiles of criminal suspects who were never convicted of a crime. Since 2004, anyone aged 10 years or over arrested in England or Wales for a "recordable offense" must provide a DNA sample to law enforcement officials. Certain information from their DNA—known as the DNA profile—is then stored electronically in the National DNA Database. Containing 4.5 million DNA profiles, it was until recently the world's largest DNA databank. Today, that distinction goes to the United States, where state and federal law enforcement databases combined contain about 5.6 million DNA profiles. Although the overwhelming majority of the DNA profiles in the United States are from convicted felons, a growing number are from parolees, probationers, and people under arrest.

Like a fingerprint, DNA is a type of bioinformation that can be used to identify people and is therefore a valuable tool in attempts to identify criminal offenders. Yet compelling persons to provide their DNA to law enforcement agencies raises concerns about informed consent, individual and familial privacy, the use of genetic information in the criminal justice system, and the retention and use of DNA profiles and samples.

Collecting DNA

In 1988 Colorado became the first state to require some criminals—in this case sex offenders—to provide a DNA sample to law enforcement officials. Two years later Virginia enacted a law requiring all convicted felons to provide DNA. States initially collected DNA samples only from persons convicted of certain sex offenses and serious violent crimes under the assumption that these individuals were likely to be repeat offenders. It was also assumed that DNA might be the only biological evidence obtained at a crime scene.

Since then, states have expanded the categories of persons required to provide a DNA sample to law enforcement officials. Today, all states collect DNA from sex offenders, and 44 states collect it from all felony offenders. Kentucky is one of 31 states that collect DNA from juveniles convicted of certain crimes. The state's court of appeals recently upheld a portion of the law that requires collecting DNA from juveniles convicted of felony sex offenses, though it ruled as unconstitutional the portion that allowed for DNA collection from juveniles convicted of burglary. Over a third of the states also permit DNA collection from individuals convicted of certain misdemeanors. For instance, New Jersey permits DNA collection for misdemeanor offenses with a prison sentence of six months or more. Several states also collect DNA samples from some probationers and parolees, and 13 states have laws that compel persons to provide a DNA sample at the time of arrest. California, Kansas, and North Dakota have the broadest arrestee laws; they require a DNA sample from everyone arrested for any felony offense. Arrestee laws with a narrower scope include New Mexico's, which authorizes DNA collection from persons arrested only for specific violent felonies.

State lawmakers continue to introduce bills to expand the categories of persons required to provide their DNA to law enforcement officials. In 2007 alone, 91 DNA expansion bills were introduced in 36 states. Almost half of the bills were aimed at people arrested for certain offenses. A total of 15 bills were passed in 12 states, though an arrestee bill in South Carolina never became law because two separate House votes failed to override the governor's veto. Of the 14 bills that became law, four authorize law enforcement officials to obtain a DNA sample from persons arrested for various felony offenses.

Congress authorized the collection of DNA samples for certain federal offenders under the DNA Analysis Backlog Elimination Act of 2000. The Act requires individuals in federal custody and those convicted of certain violent crimes who were probationers, parolees, or on supervised release to provide a DNA sample. The 2001 U.S.A. Patriot Act added additional categories of qualifying federal offenses, and the Justice for All Act of 2004 further expanded the definition of qualifying offenders to include all persons convicted of felonies under federal law.

Two recent federal actions again expanded DNA sample categories. When Congress renewed the Violence Against Women Act in 2006, it included an amendment that authorizes federal officials to collect DNA samples from individuals who are arrested and from non-United States persons detained under U.S. authority. (Non-United States persons are neither U.S. citizens nor lawful permanent resident aliens.) In April 2008 the Department of Justice published a proposed rule directing certain U.S. law enforcement agencies to collect DNA samples from individuals who are arrested, facing charges, or convicted, and from non-United States persons who are detained under U.S. authority.

State and federal courts have upheld the constitutionality of some DNA statutes—including the DNA Analysis Backlog Elimination Act of 2000 and the Justice for All Act of 2004—on the grounds that the laws do not violate privacy rights or federal constitutional protections against unreasonable searches and seizures. However, in late 2006, the Minnesota court of appeals invalidated a portion of that state's DNA arrestee law. The court ruled that the privacy interest of a person charged with, but not convicted of, an offense outweighs the state's interest in that person's DNA. To compel someone who has not been convicted of a crime to provide a DNA sample, the court ruled that law enforcement officials must first obtain a warrant based on probable cause. To date, the U.S. Supreme Court has not ruled on the constitutionality of DNA collection laws.

The DNA Profile

State and federal forensic laboratories analyze DNA samples to obtain DNA profiles of people, and these profiles are stored in various electronic databases. The National DNA Index System (NDIS) contains the DNA profiles submitted by state and federal laboratories. The FBI's [Federal Bureau of Investigation's] software program CODIS (Combined DNA Index System) links the profiles in these databases. For there to be a CODIS "hit," two DNA profiles must be perfect matches on 13 regions, or loci, of the individuals' DNA.

There is a growing dispute about whether the CODIS core loci constitute "junk DNA"—segments of genetic code that provide no information about a person's physical characteristics (phenotype) or medical conditions. Several commentators raise concerns that advances in genetic testing technologies might eventually make it possible to obtain statistical approximations of an individual's ancestry, addictive behaviors, sexual orientation, temperament, and other personal information from the genetic markers that make up the CODIS core loci. For instance, several attempts have been made to construct phenotypic profiles of criminal suspects using a new method of DNA analysis that purports to provide an inference of genetic heritage or ancestry. Obtaining such sensitive information from DNA samples collected without a person's consent raises individual and familial privacy issues, especially if

Personalized and Precise

U.S. courts have consistently found that the collection and analysis of one's DNA constitutes a "search" for two reasons. First, bodily (or at least tissue) intrusion is necessary for DNA extraction. Second, there is a substantial and uniquely personalized nature in the information contained in the DNA itself, thereby triggering protections guaranteed under the Fourth Amendment. At the same time, though, courts have upheld the operation of convicted-offender DNA databanks—including the forcible extraction and banking of DNA—for one of two reasons: because the government's interest is one of "special needs, beyond the normal need for law enforcement" or because convicted felons have a "diminished expectation" of privacy, as balanced against society's need to promote law and order.

Tania Simoncelli and Sheldon Krimsky,
American Constitution Society for Law and Policy,
August 2007.

samples collected for law enforcement purposes are released to others for research purposes. Another privacy issue is the possibility that new technologies will be able to extract medical information from DNA profiles collected for law enforcement purposes.

A Hypothetical Scenario

New Orleans [Louisiana] police collect a DNA sample from Anthony, a 16-year-old high school student arrested for allegedly assaulting his schoolteacher. However, the prosecutor does not bring charges against Anthony because the police investigation revealed that he was helping the teacher defend herself against an attack by another student. Even though Anthony was never charged with a crime, his DNA profile remains in the state's DNA database, and his DNA sample stays in storage because state law permits samples of arrestees to be retained indefinitely.

A year later, police obtain DNA samples from a homicide scene and get a partial match to Anthony's DNA profile; his DNA profile shares seven of the genetic markers of a profile in an offender DNA profile database. Thus, the partial match suggests that the crime scene DNA came from a genetic male relative. Using partial matches to support police investigations is known as "familial searching." This practice was used 115 times in the United Kingdom in 2006. Whether law enforcement agencies in other countries use this practice—and if they do, to what extent—is unknown.

Until recently, the FBI prohibited the release of identifying information attached to a DNA profile unless there was a complete CODIS match. However, in the summer of 2006, the agency issued an interim plan to release identifiable information from NDIS-participating laboratories when CODIS revealed a partial match. Some state crime labs have used partial matches, and at least two states (New York and Massachusetts) have laws permitting their databases to generate partial match profiles. In March 2008 the FBI held a symposium to address the privacy implications of familial searching. Representatives from law enforcement agencies and prosecutors offices argued that the practice should be used because it provides investigative leads that can result in arrests and convictions. Civil liberty and privacy advocates raised concerns about innocent people being put under what has been called "genetic surveillance" solely because they have a genetic relative whose DNA profile is in a law enforcement database.

After getting a partial match, New Orleans police ask Anthony's male relatives to give them a DNA sample voluntarily. Asking a certain population—such as all men in a geographic area—to provide a DNA sample to law enforcement officials is known as a DNA dragnet. Since 1987, at least 20 DNA dragnets have been conducted in the United States. Critics charge that in some communities the police have harassed individuals who refused to participate, and in one community the police obtained a warrant to collect DNA from a man after he declined to participate in a dragnet. In 2006, a federal appeals court ruled that the police violated the man's constitutional rights because they did not have probable cause to obtain a warrant to seize his DNA.

Anthony's male relatives refuse to give police DNA samples, and the local judge refuses to issue a warrant compelling them to do so. As a consequence, the police follow the male relatives in the hope of getting discarded items like cigarette butts, coffee cups, and gum wrappers from which they hope to obtain a DNA sample. This "backdoor" method of collecting DNA raises questions about whether people under surveillance have a constitutional expectation of privacy concerning their abandoned DNA, which would mean that collecting the DNA without a warrant would be a violation of the Fourth Amendment's protection against unreasonable seizures. Sometimes referred to as "surreptitious sampling," this practice reportedly is growing in popularity in law enforcement agencies throughout the country.

Police Tactics Grow More Invasive

While the police conduct their investigation, the state forensic laboratory uses new technology to analyze the crime scene DNA. The analysis suggests that the DNA is from a 20-to-30-year-old male of primarily African ancestry who has asthma and a genetic predisposition to hypertension. Four of Anthony's cousins partially fit this description. The police go to local hospitals, clinics, and pharmacies to obtain his cousins' medical records to see if one of the men has been treated for asthma or high blood pressure. The federal privacy rule under the Health Insurance Portability and Accountability Act of 1996 (HIPAA) permits hospitals, clinics, pharmacies, and other entities covered by the rule to disclose to law enforcement officials the medical, injury, and treatment information of a criminal suspect.

Based on information obtained from medical and pharmacy records, the police get warrants to arrest two of Anthony's cousins. Because Louisiana has an arrestee DNA law, the cousins are required to give the police a DNA sample. The oldest cousin's DNA matches the DNA sample from the crime scene. After the cousin is charged with murder, he demands an independent analysis of his DNA to see if it can refute the state's claim. When the new DNA analysis confirms the state's finding, the cousin demands new genetic tests that might show whether he has a genetic predisposition to violence. No reliable data are available about how many criminal defendants have tried to "argue genetics" against charges of criminal offenses or to mitigate punishment, although reports in the media and the legal literature suggest the number is low. These reports also indicate that judges have refused to let defendants use genetic information at trial, although at least one defendant was permitted to introduce it at sentencing.

Moreover, arguing genetics has implications beyond its use at trial and sentencing. Several commentators have suggested that genetic-based crime control strategies might include mandatory genetic screening to identify individuals predisposed to certain behaviors or deemed genetically predisposed to criminal offending. They might also include mandatory preventive treatment such as gene therapy or preventive detention policies. These and other potential crime control strategies raise questions about the ethical, legal, and social implications of new applications of genetic screening, about the loss of privacy and liberty for individuals identified as "genetically predisposed" to criminal offending, and about the potential for policies and practices that stigmatize and discriminate against such individuals.

Meanwhile, Anthony and his cousin who was not charged want the state to destroy their DNA samples and to remove their profiles from its DNA database. State laws about retaining DNA samples and DNA profiles vary, and there is no national standard or guideline on the matter. Some commentators raise concerns that stored DNA samples and profiles collected for law enforcement purposes will be used for genetic research to examine whether there are genetic predictors of aggression, pedophilia, mental illness, and drug and alcohol addiction. Others contend that there are valid reasons for state and federal authorities to retain DNA samples and profiles, and that adequate safeguards are in place to limit access to them and disclosure of the information they contain. To date, the law on the matter remains inconclusive.

| "The primary purpose of drug testing is not to punish students who use drugs but to prevent drug abuse and to help students already using to become drug-free."

Drug Testing Can Protect Students

National Institute on Drug Abuse

In the following viewpoint, the National Institute on Drug Abuse (NIDA) claims that drug testing in schools is an effective tool in substance abuse prevention and intervention. Drug testing helps to achieve this goal in two ways, according to NIDA: It serves as a deterrent and as a way to identify and refer youths with addiction problems to treatment and counseling. So far, the institute states that random drug testing is legal for middle and high school students involved in sports and other extracurricular activities, but laws vary by state. NIDA is a part of the National Institutes of Health.

As you read, consider the following questions:

1. In NIDA's view, what should the consequences of a positive drug test be for a student?

National Institute on Drug Abuse (NIDA), "Frequently Asked Questions About Drug Testing in Schools," September 2007. www.drugabuse.gov. Reproduced by permission.

2. Why should adolescents be tested for drugs, as stated by NIDA?

3. According to the author, how do students try to beat drug testing?

Some schools, hospitals, or places of employment conduct drug testing. There are a number of ways this can be done, including: pre-employment testing, random testing, reasonable suspicion/cause testing, post-accident testing, return to duty testing, and follow-up testing. This usually involves collecting urine samples to test for drugs such as marijuana, cocaine, amphetamines, PCP [phencyclidine], and opiates.

Following models established in the workplace, some schools have initiated random drug testing and/or reasonable suspicion/cause testing. During random testing schools select, using a random process (like flipping a coin), one or more individuals from the student population to undergo drug testing. Currently, random drug testing can only be conducted among students who participate in competitive extracurricular activities. Reasonable suspicion/cause testing involves a school requiring a student to provide a urine specimen when there is sufficient evidence to suggest that the student may have used an illicit substance. Typically, this involves the direct observations made by school officials that a student has used or possesses illicit substances, exhibits physical symptoms of being under the influence, and has patterns of abnormal or erratic behavior.

Testing Teenagers

Why do some schools want to conduct random drug tests?

Schools that have adopted random student drug testing are hoping to decrease drug abuse among students via two routes. First, schools that conduct testing hope that random testing will serve as a deterrent, and give students a reason to resist peer pressure to take drugs. Secondly, drug testing can identify adolescents who have started using drugs so that interventions can occur early, or identify adolescents who already have drug problems, so they can be referred for treatment. Drug abuse not only interferes with a student's ability to learn, but it can also disrupt the teaching environment, affecting other students as well.

Is student drug testing a stand-alone solution, or do schools need other programs to prevent and reduce drug use?

Drug testing should never be undertaken as a stand-alone response to a drug problem. If testing is done, it should be a component of broader prevention, intervention and treatment programs, with the common goal of reducing students' drug use.

If a student tests positive for drugs, should that student face disciplinary consequences?

The primary purpose of drug testing is not to punish students who use drugs but to prevent drug abuse and to help students already using to become drug-free. The results of a positive drug test should be used to intervene with students who do not yet have drug problems, through counseling and follow-up testing. For students that are diagnosed with addiction, parents and a school administrator can refer them to effective drug treatment programs, to begin the recovery process.

Why test teenagers at all?

Teens are especially vulnerable to drug abuse, when the brain and body are still developing. Most teens do not use drugs, but for those who do, it can lead to a wide range of adverse effects on the brain, the body, behavior and health.

Short term: Even a single use of an intoxicating drug can affect a person's judgment and decisionmaking—resulting in accidents, poor performance in a school or sports activity, unplanned risky behavior, and the risk of overdosing.

Long term: Repeated drug abuse can lead to serious problems, such as poor academic outcomes, mood changes

Drug-Free Role Models

Student athletes and students in extracurricular activities take leadership roles in the school community and, as role models, should be drug free—and student drug testing helps ensure this. More importantly, it gives students in extracurricular activities an "out" or an argument that they can use when pressured to take drugs (e.g., "If I take drugs, they will know because I have to take a drug test, and I'll be kicked off the team").

Drug Free America Foundation, n.d. www.dfaf.org.

(depending on the drug: depression, anxiety, paranoia, psychosis), and social or family problems caused or worsened by drugs.

Repeated drug use can also lead to the disease of *addiction*. Studies show that the earlier a teen begins using drugs, the more likely he or she will develop a substance abuse problem or addiction. Conversely, if teens stay away from drugs while in high school, they are less likely to develop a substance abuse problem later in life.

How many students actually use drugs?

Drug use among high school students has dropped significantly since 2001. In December, the 2007 Monitoring the Future study of 8th, 10th, and 12th graders showed that drug use had declined by 24 percent since 2001.

Despite this marked decline, much remains to be done. Almost 50 percent of 12th graders say that they've used drugs at least once in their lifetime, and 18 percent report using marijuana in the last month. Prescription drug abuse is high—with nearly 1 in 10 high school seniors reporting non-medical use of the prescription painkiller Vicodin in the past year.

Testing Methods

What testing methods are available?

There are several testing methods available that use urine, hair, oral fluids, and sweat (patch). These methods vary in cost, reliability, drugs detected, and detection period. Schools can determine their needs and choose the method that best suits their requirements, as long as the testing kits are from a reliable source.

Which drugs can be tested for?

Various testing methods normally test for a "panel" of drugs. Typically, a drug panel tests for marijuana, cocaine, opioids, amphetamines, and PCP. If a school has a particular problem with other drugs, such as MDMA [Ecstasy], GHB [a depressant], or steroids, they can include testing for these drugs as well.

What about alcohol?

Alcohol is a drug, and its use is a serious problem among young people. However, alcohol does not remain in the blood long enough for most tests to detect recent use. Breathalyzers and oral fluid tests can detect current use. Adolescents with substance abuse problems are often polydrug users (they use more than one drug) so identifying a problem with an illicit or prescription drug may also suggest an alcohol problem.

How accurate are drug tests? Is there a possibility a test could give a false positive?

Tests are very accurate but not 100 percent accurate. Usually samples are divided so if an initial test is positive a confirmation test can be conducted. Federal guidelines are in place to ensure accuracy and fairness in drug testing programs.

Can students "beat" the tests?

Many drug-using students are aware of techniques that supposedly detoxify their systems or mask their drug use. Popular magazines and Internet sites give advice on how to dilute urine samples, and there are even companies that sell clean urine or products designed to distort test results. A number of techniques and products are focused on urine tests for marijuana, but masking products increasingly are becoming available for tests of hair, oral fluids, and multiple drugs.

Most of these products do not work, are very costly, are easily identified in the testing process and need to be on hand constantly, because of the very nature of random testing. Moreover, even if the specific drug is successfully masked, the product itself can be detected, in which case the student using it would become an obvious candidate for additional screening and attention. In fact, some testing programs label a test "positive" if a masking product is detected.

Laws May Vary by Location

Is random drug testing of students legal?

In June 2002, the U.S. Supreme Court broadened the authority of public schools to test students for illegal drugs. Voting 5 to 4 in *Pottawatomie County v. Earls,* the court ruled to allow random drug tests for all middle and high school students participating in competitive extracurricular activities. The ruling greatly expanded the scope of school drug testing, which previously had been allowed only for student athletes.

Just because the U.S. Supreme Court said student drug testing for adolescents in competitive extracurricular activities is constitutional, does that mean it is legal in my city or state?

A school or school district that is interested in adopting a student drug testing program should seek legal expertise so that it complies with all federal, state, and local laws. Individual state constitutions may dictate different legal thresholds for allowing student drug testing. Communities interested in starting student drug testing programs should become familiar with the law in their respective states to ensure proper compliance.

What has research determined about the utility of random drug tests in schools?

There is not very much research in this area, and the early research shows mixed results. A study published in 2007 [in the *Journal of Adolescent Health*] found that student athletes who participated in randomized drug testing had overall rates of drug use similar to students who did not take part in the program, and in fact some indicators of future drug abuse increased among those participating in the drug testing program. Because of the limited number of studies on this topic more research is warranted.

> "Students are assumed guilty until they can produce a clean urine sample with no regard for their privacy rights."

Drug Testing Violates Students' Privacy

Jennifer Kern, Fatema Gunja, Alexandra Cox, Marsha Rosenbaum, Judith Appel, and Anjuli Verma

In the following viewpoint, the authors, Jennifer Kern, Fatema Gunja, Alexandra Cox, Marsha Rosenbaum, Judith Appel, and Anjuli Verma, maintain that random drug testing in schools invades privacy and is counterproductive. They allege that drug testing erodes students' trust in faculty and administrators and discourages participation in extracurricular activities. And to eliminate the possibility of false positives, students are forced to identify the prescription drugs they take, the authors contend. Ultimately, they conclude that random drug testing has the unintended consequences of misbehavior and undermining constitutional rights. The viewpoint authors are social scientists and the authors of the second edition of Making Sense of Student Drug Testing: Why Educators Are Saying No.

Jennifer Kern, Fatema Gunja, Alexandra Cox, Marsha Rosenbaum, Judith Appel, and Anjuli Verma, *Making Sense of Student Drug Testing: Why Educators Are Saying No.* Santa Cruz, CA: American Civil Liberties Union/Drug Law Reform Project, and New York, NY: Drug Policy Alliance, 2006. Reproduced by permission.

As you read, consider the following questions:

1. As told by the authors, why is drug testing for steroids ineffective?

2. Why is random drug testing of students who participate in extracurricular activities not appropriate, in the authors' view?

3. What is a better method of detecting drug abuse in schools, in the authors' opinion?

Proponents assert the success of random student drug testing by citing a handful of reports from schools that anecdotally claim drug testing reduced drug use. The only formal study to claim a reduction in drug use was based on a snapshot of two schools and was suspended by the federal government for lack of sound methodology.

In a 2005 report evaluating the available evidence, Professor Neil McKeganey critiqued the methodology and biases of the studies repeatedly presented in support of random student drug testing, saying, "It is a matter of concern that student drug testing has been widely developed within the USA . . . on the basis of the slimmest available research evidence."

Studies Do Not Support Student Testing

The first large-scale national study on student drug testing found virtually no difference in rates of drug use between schools that have drug testing programs and those that do not. Based on data collected between 1998 and 2001 from 76,000 students nationwide in 8th, 10th and 12th grades, the study found that drug testing did not have an impact on illicit drug use among students, including athletes.

Dr. Lloyd D. Johnston, an author of the study, directs *Monitoring the Future*, the leading survey by the federal government of trends in student drug use and attitudes about drugs. According to Dr. Johnston, "[The study] suggests that there really isn't an impact from drug testing as practiced . . . I don't think it brings about any constructive changes in their attitudes about drugs or their belief in the dangers associated with using them." Published in the April 2003 *Journal of School Health*, the study was conducted by researchers at the University of Michigan and funded in part by the National Institute on Drug Abuse (NIDA).

The researchers at the University of Michigan conducted a more extensive study later that year with an enlarged sample of schools, an additional year of data and an increased focus on random testing programs. The updated results reinforced their previous conclusions:

> So, does drug testing prevent or inhibit student drug use? Our data suggest that, as practiced in recent years in American secondary schools, it does not . . . The two forms of drug testing that are generally assumed to be most promising for reducing student drug use—random testing applied to all students . . . and testing of athletes—did not produce encouraging results.

The follow-up study was published in 2003 as part of the Youth, Education and Society (YES) Occasional Papers Series sponsored by the Robert Wood Johnson Foundation.

The strongest predictor of student drug use, the studies' authors note, is students' attitudes toward drug use and their perceptions of peer use. The authors recommend policies that address "these key values, attitudes and perceptions" as effective alternatives to drug testing. The results of these national studies are supported by numerous other surveys and studies that examine the effectiveness of various options for the prevention of student drug misuse. . . .

Damaging and Expensive

Drug testing can undermine student-teacher relationships by pitting students against the teachers and coaches who test them, eroding trust and leaving students ashamed and resentful.

As educators know, student-teacher trust is critical to creating an atmosphere in which students can address their fears and concerns about drug use itself, as well as the issues that can lead to drug use, including depression, anxiety, peer pressure and unstable family life. Trust is jeopardized if teachers act as confidants in some circumstances but as police in others.

Drug testing also results in missed classroom instruction. Officials at some schools with testing programs reported that many students would flagrantly ridicule the testing process by stalling for hours to produce a urine sample—during which time they remained absent from class.

Drug testing costs schools an average of $42 per student tested, which amounts to $21,000 for a high school testing 500 students. This figure is for the initial test alone and does not include the costs of other routine components of drug testing, such as additional tests throughout the year or follow-up testing.

The cost of drug testing often exceeds the total a school district spends on existing drug education, prevention and counseling programs combined. In fact, drug testing may actually take scarce resources away from the very health and treatment services needed by students who are misusing drugs.

The process for dealing with a positive test is usually long and involved; not only must a second test be done to rule out a false positive result, but treatment referral and follow-up systems must also be in place. In one school district, the cost of detecting the 11 students who tested positive amounted to $35,000.

Beyond the initial costs, there are long-term operational and administrative expenses associated with student drug testing, including:

- Monitoring students' urination to collect accurate samples;

- Documentation, bookkeeping and compliance with confidentiality requirements; and

- Tort or other insurance to safeguard against potential lawsuits.

Not All Drug Testing Is Legal

In 2002, by a margin of five to four, the U.S. Supreme Court in *Board of Education of Pottawatomie v. Earls* permitted public school districts to drug test students participating in competitive extracurricular activities. In its ruling, however, the Court only interpreted *federal* law. Schools are also subject to *state* law, which may provide greater protections for students' privacy rights. These laws vary greatly from state to state and, in many states, the law may not yet be well-defined by the courts.

Since the 2002 *Earls* decision, lawsuits have been filed in many states, including Indiana, New Jersey, Oregon, Pennsylvania, Texas and Washington, challenging school districts' drug testing policies. Most of these school districts will spend thousands of taxpayer dollars battling these lawsuits with no guarantee of success.

Addressing Steroids

The use of anabolic steroids and other performance enhancing supplements by professional athletes has prompted legislators and other policymakers to address steroid use among adolescents. On the surface, random drug testing appears to be a viable, effective deterrent to many. Research, however, does not support this approach. As with other forms of drug testing, those targeting steroids have not proven to be an effective means of reducing use. Further, steroid testing impairs the relationship of trust between students, parents, coaches and other school administrators.

Most steroid tests do not detect other performance enhancing supplements, and the more substances that are added to a test, the higher the cost. Also, testing does not reach all of those adolescents who are using steroids, as more than one-third of adolescent users do not participate in school sports. For those who do participate in sports, testing is a poor substitute for learning and appreciating the value of fair play.

The average test ranges from $100 to $200 per test. The New Orleans *Times-Picayune* reported that a local coach estimated steroid tests for his football team would cost $7,000. He commented, "And I have a budget of $9,000. You know what [drug testing] would do to sports at this school? It would shut us down." As Robert F. Kanaby, Executive Director of the National Federation of State High School Associations, observes, "We must recognize that in an era of scarce resources, steroid testing is way down on [the] budgetary pecking order for most school districts. This is particularly true if there is another good way to address the problem, and there is." . . .

Preventing Extracurricular Activities

Random drug testing is typically directed at students who want to participate in extracurricular activities, including athletics, which have proven among the most effective pathways to preventing adolescent drug use. However, all too often drug testing policies actually prevent students from engaging in these activities.

Research shows a vastly disproportionate incidence of adolescent drug use and other dangerous behavior occurs during the unsupervised hours between the end of classes and parents' arrival home in the evening.

Research also shows that students who participate in extracurricular activities are:

- Less likely to develop substance abuse problems;

- Less likely to engage in other dangerous behavior such as violent crime; and

- More likely to stay in school, earn higher grades, and set and achieve more ambitious educational goals.

In addition, after-school programs offer students who are experimenting with or misusing drugs productive activities as well as contact with teachers, coaches and peers, who can help them identify and address problematic drug use.

The Tulia [Texas] Independent School District, one of the many districts facing heightened public concerns about privacy and confidentiality, has seen a dramatic reduction in student participation in extracurricular activities since implementing drug testing. One female student explains:

> I know lots of kids who don't want to get into sports and stuff because they don't want to get drug tested. That's one of the reasons I'm not into any [activity]. Cause ... I'm on medication, so I would always test positive, and then they would have to ask me about my medication, and I would be embarrassed. And what if I'm on my period? I would be too embarrassed.

False Positives Punish Innocent Students

A positive drug test can be a devastating accusation for an innocent student. The most widely used drug screening method, urinalysis, will falsely identify some students as illicit drug users when they are not actually using illicit drugs, because drug testing does not necessarily distinguish between drug metabolites with similar structures. For example:

- Over-the-counter decongestants may produce a positive result for amphetamine.

- Codeine can produce a positive result for heroin.

- Food products with poppy seeds can produce a positive result for opiates.

Out of a desire to eliminate the possibility for false positives, schools often ask students to identify their prescription medications before taking a drug test. This both compromises students' privacy rights and creates an added burden for schools to ensure that students' private information is safely guarded.

Drug testing says very little about who is misusing or abusing drugs. Thousands of students might be tested in order to detect a tiny fraction of those who may have used the drugs covered by the test. Additionally students misusing other harmful substances not detected by drug tests will not be identified. If schools rely on drug testing, they may undervalue better ways of detecting young people who are having problems with drugs. Most often, problematic drug use is discovered by learning to recognize its common symptoms. Properly trained teachers, coaches and other school officials can identify symptoms of a potential drug problem by paying attention to such signs as student absences, erratic behavior, changes in grades and withdrawal from peers.

Unintended Consequences

Students may turn to more dangerous drugs or binge drinking. Because marijuana is the most detectable drug, with traces of THC remaining in the body for weeks, students may simply take drugs that exit the body quickly, like methamphetamine, MDMA (Ecstasy) or inhalants. Knowing alcohol is less detectable, they may also engage in binge drinking, creating health and safety risks for students and the community as a whole.

Students can outsmart the drug test. Students who fear being caught by a drug test may find ways to cheat the test, often by purchasing products on the Internet. A quick Internet search for "pass drug test" yields nearly four million hits, linking students to websites selling drug-free replacement urine, herbal detoxifiers, hair follicle shampoo and other products designed to beat drug tests. Students may also try dangerous home remedies. The president of the school board for Guymon, Oklahoma, described a frantic parent who had caught her daughter drinking bleach; the district's drug testing program was subsequently abandoned. In one Louisiana school district, students who were facing a hair test shaved their heads and body hair, making a mockery of the drug testing program.

Students learn that they are guilty until proven innocent. Students are taught that under the U.S. Constitution people are presumed innocent until proven guilty and have a reasonable expectation of privacy. Random drug testing undermines both lessons; students are assumed guilty until they can produce a clean urine sample with no regard for their privacy rights.

Periodical Bibliography

The following articles have been selected to supplement the diverse views presented in this chapter.

Richard
Alonso-Zaldivar
"Effectiveness of Medical Privacy Law Is Questioned," *Los Angeles Times*, April 9, 2008.

Aubrey Fox
"The Move to Expand DNA Testing," *Gotham Gazette*, May 2007.

David Goldberg
"Privacy, Please: HIPAA Changes Will Broaden Patient Protection," *Dermatology Times*, December 1, 2009.

Amy Harmon
"Defense Lawyers Fight DNA Samples Gained on Sly," *New York Times*, April 3, 2008.

Larry Hartstein
and Todd Holcomb
"Drug Testing by High Schools Gets a Push From QB's Death," *Atlanta Journal-Constitution*, July 10, 2007.

Stuart Jeffries
"Suspect Nation," *Guardian* (Manchester, UK), October 28, 2006. www.guardian.co.uk.

Donna Leinwan
"Principal: Drug-Testing Students Works," *USA Today*, July 12, 2006.

Chris A. MacKinnon
"Regulated to the Hilt," *Processor*, May 8, 2009.

Ellen Nakashima
and Spencer Hsu
"U.S. to Expand Collection Of Crime Suspects' DNA," *Washington Post*, April 17, 2008.

Eddy Ramirez
"When a Positive Is a Negative," *St. Petersburg (FL) Times*, October 2, 2006.

Rebecca Waters
"Expanded DNA Databases: Violation of Privacy or Crime Solving Tool?" *Forensic Magazine*, May 7, 2009.

CHAPTER 4

How Should Privacy Be Protected?

Chapter Preface

Although eighteen-year-old Nikki Catsouras died on Halloween in 2006, the horror of her fatal car crash lives on on the Internet, agonizing her family. Nine digital photos of the shocking scene leaked by California Highway Patrol (CHP) officers went viral; only a few days following Nikki's death, her father received an e-mail containing a snapshot of the wreck and her lifeless face covered in blood, captioned with "Woohoo Daddy! Hey daddy, I'm still alive."[1] The rest of Nikki's family were also sent anonymous texts and e-mails with the pictures.

A strikingly pretty college freshman from a well-heeled southern California community, Nikki had taken her father's Porsche after a fight with him and lost control of the car, smashing into a tollbooth at a speed of 100 miles per hour. The autopsy revealed that she had small amounts of cocaine in her system. These circumstances brought out the worst of online hoaxsters, who set up a false MySpace profile of her. User comments disparaged Nikki as a "spoiled rich girl" and the tragedy "a waste of a Porsche."[2] The graphic photos also wound up on Web sites trading in obscene and exploitative content, dubbing her the "Porsche Girl."

Nikki's parents took to the ceaseless removal of the images from the Internet and forbade their children from going online. They also sued the CHP and the two officers who were purportedly behind the leak, Aaron Reich and Thomas O'Donnell, for invasion of privacy, negligence, and intentional infliction of emotional distress. While the photos were taken as a standard procedure in accidents, Reich and O'Donnell violated a policy and forwarded the photos in e-mails. A judge

1. *Newsweek*, May 4, 2009.
2. *Newsweek*, May 4, 2009.

dismissed the case, though, citing the lack of legal protection for the family because privacy rights do not explicitly extend to the deceased. The California Court of Appeal reversed the decision in February 2010, ruling that the Catsourases had a right to pursue the latter of the two charges against Reich and O'Donnell.

"The case . . . illustrates how the law has struggled to define how legal concepts like privacy and defamation are translated into an online world,"[3] wrote Jessica Bennett in a feature on the Catsourases in *Newsweek*. In the following chapter, the authors debate how privacy may or may not be protected.

3. *Newsweek*, May 4, 2009.

| *"The government could argue persuasively that the release of [student] information serves a compelling state interest in facilitating the maintenance of the nation's armed forces."*

Military Recruiters Should Be Permitted to Access Students' Information

Jody Feder

In the following viewpoint, Jody Feder defends the recruitment methods of the military. Under the current law, high schools that receive federal funds must grant military recruiters access to students equal to private employers and universities and colleges, she states, as well as provide student names, addresses, and telephone numbers upon request. Still, Feder maintains that personal information such as Social Security numbers or medical records are protected, and parents and students are given notice of the release of information and can opt out. Feder is a legislative attorney for the American Law Division of the Congressional Research Service, Library of Congress.

Jody Feder, "Military Recruitment Provisions Under the No Child Left Behind Act: A Legal Analysis," CRS Report for Congress, January 8, 2008, pp. 1–5.

As you read, consider the following questions:

1. According to the author, what are opponents' contentions to the current recruitment provisions?

2. As described by Feder, how do schools interpret "opt out" provisions?

3. In Feder's opinion, why would a court not hold an expectation of privacy for basic contact information?

When Congress enacted the No Child Left Behind Act (NCLBA) of 2001, it added several new requirements regarding the ability of military recruiters to access student information and to approach students directly. These new provisions—which are different from similar Department of Defense (DOD) provisions that allow DOD to compile directory information on high school students for military recruitment purposes or that require colleges and universities that receive federal funds to allow military recruiters on campus—have proven to be somewhat controversial. Proponents of the recruitment provisions argue that the new law allows recruiters to inform students about the military opportunities available to them and eases the task of recruiting volunteers to sustain the nation's military forces. On the other hand, opponents contend that the provisions raise concerns about student privacy and should be changed to make it easier to opt out. Currently, 95% of the country's school districts are estimated to be complying with the new requirements, although it is important to note that, traditionally, most schools had already allowed military recruiters to contact students long before the NCLBA provisions became mandatory.

The new NCLBA military recruitment provisions require high schools that receive federal funds to meet two requirements. First, such schools must "provide, on a request made by military recruiters . . . , access to secondary school students names, addresses, and telephone listings," and second, schools must "provide military recruiters the same access to secondary school students as is provided generally to post secondary educational institutions or to prospective employers of those students." Schools that fail to comply with either of these two requirements—access to student information or equal access to students themselves—risk losing federal funds. However, private secondary schools that maintain a religious objection to military service are exempt from the recruitment provisions.

Access to Student Information

As noted above, schools must, when requested, provide military recruiters with information concerning student names, addresses, and telephone numbers. Unlike more personal information such as Social Security numbers, this type of data is not protected by the Family Educational Rights and Privacy Act (FERPA), which currently allows the release of student directory information in the absence of parental objections. Thus, even before the NCLBA provisions were enacted, such student contact information was potentially available to outside entities.

Like FERPA, the NCLBA also provides the opportunity to opt out of the provisions requiring the release of directory information to military recruiters. Under the NCLBA, students or their parents may request that the student's directory information not be released without prior written consent. In addition, the local educational agency or private school must notify parents of their right to make such a request.

Schools appear to have interpreted these opt out provisions in a variety of ways. For example, some schools have, as part of their compliance with an array of privacy laws, issued a general notice informing parents that they can opt out of the release of student contact information, while other schools have issued a separate and more explicit notice informing parents that such information may be released to the military for recruitment purposes if the parents do not opt out. Both of

An Individual Choice

Corporal Curtis Harding, who enlisted in the Marines after high school, said every person should have the freedom to make their own choices.

"Parents should take a step back," Harding said. "Everyone always wants to tell you what to do, but in the end it is really up to the individual to decide about where they want to go in their own life. And in the military the worst that can happen is that you don't like it, so at that point you can just leave. It's simple."

Diego Cupulo, Gotham Gazette, *January 2007.*

these types of notice appear to meet the statutory requirement regarding informing parents of their right to opt out, but recipients of the latter type of notice may be more likely to exercise that option. As a result, the type of notice that a school elects to provide has been a subject of debate.

In addition, the notification provision has become controversial in part because schools have interpreted parental responses in different ways. For example, if parents fail to respond to the notice informing them of their right to opt out of the release of student information, some schools interpret the lack of response as indicating that the parent does not wish to opt out, while other schools interpret a lack of response as signifying that the parent does want to opt out. As a result, some interest groups have pressed legislators to clarify the law with regard to this point.

Equal Access to Students

In addition to requiring schools to provide access to student information, the NCLBA also requires schools to provide access to students themselves. Specifically, schools must provide military recruiters the same access to students as is otherwise provided to other recruiters, such as private employers or institutions of higher education. As with the notification provisions, schools have implemented the equal access provisions in a variety of ways. For example, some schools allow extensive access, permitting recruiters to set up information tables, visit classrooms, and freely approach students anywhere on campus. Other schools permit a lesser degree of access, and some restrict military access even further by forbidding information tables, requiring appointments before recruiters can meet students, and otherwise limiting access to campus. Despite these variations in school policy, schools are allowed to place as many or as few restrictions as they wish on military recruiters, as long as schools treat such recruiters the same way they treat other entities that wish to contact students.

Legal and Privacy Concerns

As noted previously, some opponents of the NCLBA military recruitment provisions have raised legal concerns about the new requirements. In particular, some critics have questioned whether the recruitment provisions violate a student's right to privacy, but neither statutory nor constitutional analysis appears to support this argument. Indeed, from a statutory perspective, the NCLBA provisions regarding release of student contact information are, as noted above, entirely consistent with FERPA, the longstanding law that protects the educational privacy rights of students. Likewise, the NCLBA military recruitment provisions, for the reasons discussed below, do not appear to raise constitutional concerns.

Under the auspices of the Fourteenth Amendment, the Supreme Court has recognized that there is a constitutional right to privacy that protects against certain governmental disclosures of personal information, but it has not established the standard for measuring such a violation. In the absence of explicit standards, the circuit courts have tended to establish a series of balancing tests that weigh the competing privacy interests and government interests in order to determine when information privacy violations occur.

In *Falvo ex rel. Pletan v. Owasso Independent School District No. I-011*, the Court of Appeals for the Tenth Circuit weighed the plaintiff's claim that peer grading and the practice of calling out grades in class resulted in an impermissible release of her child's education records in violation of FERPA. The plaintiff also claimed that the practice of peer grading violated her child's constitutional right to privacy. Although the court, in a holding that was later reversed by the Supreme Court, ruled that the practice of peer grading violated FERPA, the Tenth Circuit denied the plaintiff's constitutional claim. In rejecting this claim, the court applied a three-part balancing test that considers "(1) if the party asserting the right has a legitimate expectation of privacy, (2) if disclosure serves a compelling state interest, and (3) if disclosure can be made in the least intrusive manner." Based on the first prong of this test, the Tenth Circuit rejected the plaintiff's constitutional claim because it ruled that student's school work and test grades were not highly personal matters that deserved constitutional protection.

A Reasonable Request for Contact

Like peer graded student homework assignments, the release of student names, addresses, and telephone numbers to military recruiters would probably not be viewed by a court as violating a student's constitutional right to privacy under such a balancing test. Unlike Social Security numbers or medical records, for example, it is unlikely that a court would hold that individuals have a legitimate expectation of privacy in the type of basic contact information that is typically found in a phone book. Furthermore, the government could argue persuasively that the release of such information serves a compelling state interest in facilitating the maintenance of the nation's armed forces. Finally, a court would probably view the disclosure required by the NCLBA as minimally intrusive, given that students can either opt out of the information release or decline to join the military, or both.

Ultimately, a court reviewing any privacy based challenge to the NCLBA military recruitment provisions would be likely to reject such a claim, especially in light of the fact that Congress was clearly acting within the scope of its constitutional authority when it enacted the military recruitment provisions of the NCLBA. Under the Spending Clause of the Constitution, Congress frequently promotes its policy goals by conditioning the receipt of federal funds on state compliance with certain requirements. Indeed, the Supreme Court "has repeatedly upheld against constitutional challenge the use of this technique to induce governments and private parties to cooperate voluntarily with federal policy," and the Court recently reaffirmed this principle when, in response to a First Amendment challenge, it upheld similar military recruitment provisions that apply to colleges that receive federal funds. Thus, the Court would likely uphold the NCLBA provisions in part on the basis of congressional authority under the Spending Clause.

> *"In the past few years, the military has mounted a virtual invasion into the lives of young Americans."*

Military Recruiters Should Be Barred from Accessing Students' Information

David Goodman

In the following viewpoint, David Goodman contends that the military uses methods of recruitment and promotion that invade the privacy of students. Through data mining, deceptive Web sites, and cunning marketing programs, the Pentagon, run by the United States Department of Defense, collects and compiles personal and detailed information from unsuspecting minors nationwide, he argues. Goodman notes that more students are opting out of sharing their information with military recruiters as the wars in the Middle East persist. Goodman is a contributing writer for Mother Jones *and coauthor of* Static: Government Liars, Media Cheerleaders, and the People Who Fight Back.

As you read, consider the following questions:

1. Why did military recruitment of students become more aggressive, as stated by the author?

David Goodman, "A Few Good Kids?" *Mother Jones*, September–October 2009. Copyright © 2009 Foundation for National Progress. Reproduced by permission.

2. How does *March2Success.com* obtain information about test takers, according to Goodman?

3. As told by Goodman, what happened when several students refused to participate in the Armed Services' Career Exploration Program?

John Travers was striding purposefully into the Westfield mall in Wheaton, Maryland, for some back-to-school shopping before starting his junior year at Bowling Green State University. When I asked him whether he'd ever talked to a military recruiter, Travers, a 19-year-old African American with a buzz cut, a crisp white T-shirt, and a diamond stud in his left ear, smiled wryly. "To get to lunch in my high school, you had to pass recruiters," he said. "It was overwhelming." Then he added, "I thought the recruiters had too much information about me. They called me, but I never gave them my phone number."

Nor did he give the recruiters his email address, Social Security number, or details about his ethnicity, shopping habits, or college plans. Yet they probably knew all that, too. In the past few years, the military has mounted a virtual invasion into the lives of young Americans. Using data mining, stealth websites, career tests, and sophisticated marketing software, the Pentagon is harvesting and analyzing information on everything from high school students' GPAs [grade point averages] and SAT [Scholastic Aptitude Test] scores to which video games they play. Before an Army recruiter even picks up the phone to call a prospect like Travers, the soldier may know more about the kid's habits than do his own parents.

The Tip of the Data Iceberg

The military has long struggled to find more effective ways to reach potential enlistees; for every new GI [soldier] it signed up last year [2008], the Army spent $24,500 on recruitment. (In contrast, four-year colleges spend an average of $2,000 per incoming student.) Recruiters hit pay dirt in 2002, when then Representative (now Senator) David Vitter (R-La.) slipped a provision into the No Child Left Behind Act [NCLB] that requires high schools to give recruiters the names and contact details of all juniors and seniors. Schools that fail to comply risk losing their NCLB funding. This little-known regulation effectively transformed [former] President George W. Bush's signature education bill into the most aggressive military recruitment tool since the draft. Students may sign an opt-out form—but not all school districts let them know about it.

Yet NCLB is just the tip of the data iceberg. In 2005, privacy advocates discovered that the Pentagon had spent the past two years quietly amassing records from Selective Service, state DMVs [Departments of Motor Vehicles], and data brokers to create a database of tens of millions of young adults and teens, some as young as 15. The massive data-mining project is overseen by the Joint Advertising Market Research & Studies [JAMRS] program, whose website has described the database, which now holds 34 million names, as "arguably the largest repository of 16–25-year-old youth data in the country." The JAMRS database is in turn run by Equifax, the credit reporting giant.

Marc Rotenberg, head of the Electronic Privacy Information Center, says the Pentagon's initial failure to disclose the collection of the information likely violated the Privacy Act. In 2007, the Pentagon settled a lawsuit (filed by the New York Civil Liberties Union) by agreeing to stop collecting the names and Social Security numbers of anyone younger than 17 and promising not to share its database records with other government agencies. Students may opt out of having their JAMRS database information sent to recruiters, but only 8,700 have invoked this obscure safeguard.

The Pentagon also spends about $600,000 a year on commercial data brokers, notably the Student Marketing Group [SMG] and the American Student List [ASL], which boasts

What If My Child Is Home-Schooled?

If the local school district has your child's contact information, then they may release that information to the military. Your local school district may have your contact information even if your child is not enrolled, especially if your child tests through the district or is registered with the district to obtain a GED [General Education Development degree] or high school diploma equivalent.

The military can also get information for its non-school-based, Pentagon database through DMV [Department of Motor Vehicle] records, consumer data, and other sources.

Leave My Child Alone, October 14, 2005.
www.leavemychildalone.org.

that it has records for 8 million high school students. Both companies have been accused of using deceptive practices to gather information: In 2002, New York's attorney general sued SMG for telling high schools it was surveying students for scholarship and financial aid opportunities yet selling the info to telemarketers; the Federal Trade Commission charged ASL with similar tactics. Both companies eventually settled.

The Pentagon is also gathering data from unsuspecting Web surfers. This year [2009], the Army spent $1.2 million on the website *March2Success.com*, which provides free standardized test-taking tips devised by prep firms such as Peterson's, Kaplan, and Princeton Review. The only indications that the Army runs the site, which registers an average of 17,000 new users each month, are a tiny tagline and a small logo that links to the main recruitment website, *GoArmy.com*. Yet visitors' contact information can be sent to recruiters unless they opt out, and students also have the option of having a recruiter monitor their practice test scores. Terry Backstrom, who runs *March2Success.com* for the US Army Recruiting Command at Fort Knox, insists that it is about "good will," not recruiting. "We are providing a great service to schools that normally would cost them."

Data Mining the Classroom

Recruiters are also data mining the classroom. More than 12,000 high schools administer the Armed Services Vocational Aptitude Battery [ASVAB], a three-hour multiple-choice test originally created in 1968 to match conscripts with military assignments. Rebranded in the mid-1990s as the "ASVAB Career Exploration Program," the test has a cheerful home page that makes no reference to its military applications, instead declaring that it "is designed to help students learn more about themselves and the world of work." A student who takes the test is asked to divulge his or her Social Security number, GPA, ethnicity, and career interests—all of which is then logged into the JAMRS database. In 2008, more than 641,000 high school students took the ASVAB; 90 percent had their scores sent to recruiters. Tony Castillo of the Army's Houston Recruiting Battalion says that ASVAB is "much more than a test to join the military. It is really a gift to public education."

Concerns about the ASVAB's links to recruiting have led to a nearly 20 percent decline in the number of test takers between 2003 and 2008. But the test is mandatory at approximately 1,000 high schools. Last February [2009], three North Carolina students were sent to detention for refusing to take it. One, a junior named Dakota Ling, told the local paper, "I just really don't want the military to have all the info it can on me." Last year, the California Legislature barred schools from sending ASVAB results to military recruiters, though Governor Arnold Schwarzenegger vetoed the bill. The Los Angeles and

Washington, DC, school districts have tried to protect students' information by releasing their scores only on request.

To put all its data to use, the military has enlisted the help of Nielsen Claritas, a research and marketing firm whose clients include BMW, AOL, and Starbucks. Last year, it rolled out a "custom segmentation" program that allows a recruiter armed with the address, age, race, and gender of a potential "lead" to call up a wealth of information about young people in the immediate area, including recreation and consumption patterns. The program even suggests pitches that might work while cold-calling teenagers. "It's just a foot in the door for a recruiter to start a relevant conversation with a young person," says Donna Dorminey of the US Army Center for Accessions Research.

Still, no amount of data slicing can fix the challenge of recruiting during wartime. Last year, a JAMRS survey identified recruiters' single biggest obstacle: Only 5 percent of parents would recommend military service to their kids, a situation blamed on "a constant barrage of negative media coverage on the War in Iraq." Not surprisingly, more and more kids are opting out of having their information shared with recruiters under No Child Left Behind; in New York City, the number of students opting out has doubled in the past five years, to 45,000 in 2008. At some schools, 90 percent of students have opted out. In 2007, JAMRS awarded a $50 million contract to Mullen Advertising to continue its marketing campaign to target "influencers" such as parents, coaches, and guidance counselors. The result: print ads that declare, "Your son wants to join the military. The question isn't whether he's prepared enough, but whether you are."

Not far from the mall in Maryland, I asked 21-year-old Marcelo Salazar, who'd been a cadet in his high school's Junior Reserve Officer Training Corps, why he'd decided not to enlist after graduating from John F. Kennedy High School in

Silver Spring, Maryland, in 2005. Now a community college student, he replied that his mother was firmly against it.

Then, as if on cue, his cell phone chirped: It was a recruiter who called him constantly. He ignored it. "War is cool," he said, flipping on his aviator sunglasses. "But if you're dying, it's not."

> *"Capturing data reflecting individual interests and habits is an enormous and growing business—evidence that consumer privacy is under siege."*

Consumer Privacy on the Internet Must Be Protected

Pamela Jones Harbour

In the following viewpoint, Pamela Jones Harbour argues that consumer privacy is endangered on the Internet. Without their consent or awareness, users' information is collected and behaviors are tracked when they use e-mail, social-networking sites, search engines, and other widely used applications, she alleges. Harbour also charges that many corporate privacy policies and practices are insufficient and offer neither disclosure nor choice. Therefore, she urges the Federal Trade Commission (FTC) to investigate developing online advertising and marketing schemes. Harbour served as a commissioner of the FTC from 2003 to 2009.

As you read, consider the following questions:

1. What happens to consumer information once it is shared, in Harbour's view?

Pamela Jones Harbour, "Remarks Before FTC Exploring Privacy Roundtable," Federal Trade Commission, December 7, 2009.www.ftc.gov.

2. How does the author back her claim that consumers care about their privacy?

3. According to John Battelle, what is the "database of intentions"?

As many of you know, my time at the FTC [Federal Trade Commission] is coming to a close. Throughout my term, privacy issues have been among my highest priorities. I am encouraged that the Commission, through this roundtable series [of December 2009], is now engaging stakeholders in a holistic discussion of privacy. The 2007 Behavioral Town Hall initiated an important conversation by focusing attention on behavioral targeting. But even more importantly, the Town Hall raised the key questions that have since triggered a return to first principles, as the FTC re-evaluates the frameworks it uses to analyze privacy.

The Need for Greater Attention to Privacy

As part of its promise of change, the current Administration has embraced technology and innovation, along with a new era of openness. But real change cannot just be aspirational. It requires concrete action. And unfortunately, with respect to privacy, I believe action has not been a high enough priority to date. I certainly do not intend to criticize Representative [Rick] Boucher's efforts to craft legislative guidance on behavioral advertising. But as I have previously stated, the United States needs comprehensive privacy legislation. If we continue the piecemeal approach to privacy in this country, we merely push aside the underlying issues.

The privacy debate goes far beyond online advertising, because behavioral targeting represents just one aspect of a multifaceted privacy conundrum. Data collection, aggregation, and use (as well as reuse, sale and resale) are driving the creation of on- and offline "digital dossiers." Capturing data reflecting individual interests and habits is an enormous and growing business—evidence that consumer privacy is under siege.

Online advertising is an enormous source of information collected about consumers, and serves as an important lens to focus our understanding of data collection and use. Most consumers cannot begin to comprehend the types and amount of information collected by businesses, or why their information may be commercially valuable. Data is currency. The larger the data set, the greater potential for analysis—and profit.

Collection of consumer data is by no means new. Census information, credit reports, and Nielsen data have existed for decades. The Internet, however, enables the creation of vastly larger quantities of consumer data. These data are collected every time we send email, update status on a social networking site, read a news article, run a search, or make an online purchase.

Of course, these technologies have the potential to offer valuable benefits to consumers. The problem, however, is that many consumers are completely unaware of the privacy implications of these services, which makes it difficult for consumers to exercise informed choices about the sites they visit and the data they disclose. In many instances, consumers pay for "free" content and services by disclosing their personal information. Their data are then used to generate targeted advertising that subsidizes online activities.

The Extent of Online Data Sharing

I am especially troubled by the asymmetry between consumer perceptions and business realities. If consumers do not comprehend how their personal information is collected and used, it is impossible for them to knowingly consent to either disclosure or use. And once data are shared, they cannot simply be recalled or deleted. The cumulative consequences for consumers are magnified, whether they realize it or not.

It is possible that small, discrete disclosures of information do not raise concerns for an individual consumer. But large aggregations of data, based on a lifetime of commercial activity, might evoke a different response. I fear we may reach a "tipping point" whereby consumers decide they want to exercise greater control over the use of their data, but their attempts to exercise control become futile, because so much of their digital life already has been exposed.

Industry attempts to provide notice and choice to consumers have been insufficient thus far. I hope we would all agree that disclosures about information collection, use, and control are not meaningful if they are buried deep within opaque privacy policies. Even if we can decipher the cryptic disclosures, they provide consumers with no meaningful access or choice, which renders those concepts largely illusory. We have strayed far from the Fair Information Practices that should serve as a baseline for any comprehensive privacy legislation.

All of this matters because consumers really do care about their personal privacy, and are willing to take steps to protect it. The findings of the Turow/Hoofnagle report [September 2009 report, "Americans Reject Tailored Advertising"] conclude that 66 percent of American adults *reject* tailored ads to begin with. That number increases to over 75 percent when consumers are actually educated about the relevant marketing techniques. Yet, companies are not delivering the privacy protections that consumers prefer.

Even where consumers have the ability to opt-out, the effects are limited. If consumer data are unavailable from one source, often they can be obtained from another. Flash cookies and other technology largely circumvent cookie controls. We may soon long for the day when all we worried about were cookies. For every company crafting a response that addresses notice, choice, or transparency, there are several more firms trying to parse and evade the intent of Commission guidance. We have entered a digital arms race, and the current outlook is troubling.

Consumer Protection and Competition

Privacy issues are important enough that the Commission should use every possible tool at its disposal. During my term as a Commissioner, I have been immersed in both consumer protection and competition issues. I have steadfastly argued that the Commission should apply its competition expertise to the privacy arena.

For example, when the Commission approved the Google/DoubleClick merger in December 2007, I wrote a dissenting statement that, among other things, highlighted the nexus between privacy and competition. While my colleagues at the time disagreed with my premise, subsequent changes in the marketplace have reinforced the validity of my concerns, as well as my premise that privacy protection is increasingly viewed as a non-price dimension of competition.

My dissent in Google/DoubleClick proposed the concept of a market for data itself, separate from markets for the services fueled by the data. The dissent discussed [journalist] John Battelle's "database of intentions" concept, which he describes as the "aggregate results of every search ever entered, every result list ever tendered, and every path taken as a result." Battelle asserts that no single company controls this collection of information, but posits that a few select companies share control. One of my key concerns in Google/DoubleClick was that the merged entity might move closer to dominating the database of intentions, and that the network effects generated by combining the two firms might have long-term negative consequences for consumers. In response to questions raised during the concurrent U.S. and EU [European Union] review of the proposed Google/DoubleClick merger, Google assured regulators that the deal was not motivated by a desire to enter the behavioral advertising market. In March of this year [2009], however, the company did in fact begin to engage in interest-based, or behavioral, advertising.

And last month [November], Google purchased mobile advertising company AdMob. This acquisition enhanced Google's ability to extend its advertising strategy into the fast-growing mobile market—an important market in which I hope, and expect, the Commission will remain vigilant.

Turbulent economic times are forcing companies to seek out new sources of revenue. Those sources are driven, in turn, by increasingly large amounts of data, as well as the ability to mine the various connections between pieces of data. As firms continue to develop new data-based markets—including, for example, cloud computing and smart grid services—we must engage in more serious inquiries regarding both the privacy and competition issues that affect consumers.

Competing to Provide Privacy Tools

It is worth noting that, to the extent one might define a putative market for consumer data, recent mergers have further concentrated the competitive landscape. It may also be the case that Comcast's announced acquisition of NBC [National Broadcasting Company] from GE [General Electric] should be analyzed from both competition and consumer protection angles.

In any event, competition on the basis of privacy protection is likely to increase as consumer awareness grows. The issues raised by data collection and use provide ripe opportunities for companies to develop pro-consumer privacy tools, and to market these features to distinguish themselves from competitors.

I know the Commission will continue to be the thought leader on privacy. I will certainly do my part to push the Commission, as I have done for six years now, by challenging mainstream opinions and asking tough questions. Wherever the conversation may lead, I am proud of the efforts of talented Commission staff, and extremely gratified that we have reached the point where we are hosting today's roundtable.

> "What consumers want isn't a secret anymore—and technology is empowering marketers to deliver."

Tracking Consumers on the Internet Can Be Beneficial

Jessica Tsai

In the following viewpoint, Jessica Tsai writes that the concept of "behavioral targeting," tracking an individual's interaction with a Web site, enables businesses to better target their audiences and give consumers what they want. Tsai claims that successful behavioral targeting can substantially increase returns and decrease the costs of advertising. For consumers, it means an end to the bombardment of unwanted online ads and offers, Tsai suggests. Nonetheless, the author states that behavioral marketing is still in development and faces technological pitfalls. Tsai is an assistant editor at CRM Magazine, *a customer-relations publication.*

As you read, consider the following questions:

1. What is a misperception about tracking customers online and privacy, according to Richard Howe?

Jessica Tsai, "Oh, Behave! It's Never Easy to Know Precisely What Your Customers Are Feeling—but You Can Certainly Pay Attention to What They're Doing, and Behavioral Targeting Can Lead to Actionable Insight," *CRM Magazine*, vol. 12, 2008, pp. 25–29. Copyright © 2008 Information Today, Inc. Reproduced by permission.

2. What may lead regulators to restrict behavioral marketing, in Tsai's view?

3. How does Richard Howe describe the future of behavioral marketing?

"I've found my perfect customers, and I know what they want." What marketer hasn't woken up having dreamt of being able to say those words? And yet even the most talented in the field have been more apt to wake up in a cold sweat instead, despite tools at their disposal such as analytics and segmentation, custom-packaged direct mail and strategic keywords. In the near future, though, marketers may awaken to a brand new day: What better way to know what consumers want than to watch how those consumers actually behave?

The concept of behavioral targeting (BT) has been around since the late '90s, disappearing for a few years after the dotcom bomb, according to Andy Chen, vice president of digital solutions for Viacom Brand Solutions International. At the time, Chen says, companies such as Engage (Flycast) and DoubleClick only "dabbled" in BT technology. Today, behavioral targeting is acting out—and experiencing a comeback.

Tapping Into Consumer's Interests

Technology has enabled marketers to tap into behavioral targeting, allowing them to watch how individuals are interacting with the online experience and to predict, in real time, the best message to launch. For all marketers, having the ability to respond "in the moment" has become a crucial strategic advantage. "Companies don't want to offer consumers products and services they don't want," says Richard Howe, chief marketing and strategy officer for data management vendor Acxiom. In the same respect, he says, "consumers are tired of getting stuff that has no relation to what they're interested in." What consumers want isn't a secret anymore—and technology is empowering marketers to deliver.

With advanced technology and a wealth of customer data, the growing importance of BT is evident by the burst of acquisitions in the space in 2007, most notably Google's move in April [2007] to acquire online advertising pioneer Double-Click for $3.1 billion in cash. If the deal goes through—[it did]—Google gains access to an incredible store of information, making it even more at the vanguard of behavioral targeting and advertising. As one industry pundit put it, "The company could know more about Web surfers than they know about themselves." In the aftermath of Google's DoubleClick announcement, other acquisitions included Yahoo! snagging BlueLithium for $300 million and AOL buying Tacoda for an undisclosed price in September. These moves and others have led observers to suggest that the next golden age of behavioral targeting is around the corner.

How far around the corner remains to be seen. Much of the industry is still lagging behind the early adopters, according to Michael Greene, research associate at JupiterResearch. In a survey of 277 online advertisers, only 16 percent reported using behavioral targeting. Whether that sounds like a good or bad result, what's interesting is that it's unchanged from the results of a similar 2004 study, when "16 percent" represented a huge jump. That year, Nate Elliot, associate analyst at JupiterResearch, noted that the share of advertisers using BT went from 10 percent in 2003 to 16 percent—a 60 percent increase. Elliot had a presciently pessimistic view, however: He was quoted at the time as saying that, with the hype and explosive growth, the area would continue to flourish, but "it'll never be a dominant force in the market." As big ad servers get in the game, he added, "the technology will be commoditized," hence making it difficult for others to rely solely on BT.

Still a Developing Technology

Three years later, that's turned out to be a solid prediction. And the future may be no better: Only 19 percent of marketers anticipate using the technology in the next 12 months. "Behavioral targeting has yet to gain broad usage, but it is certainly on the mind of a lot of online advertisers," Greene says. As more marketers embark on this new wave, they will hopefully overcome what Greene reports to be their most persistent plague—finding the right audience.

Meanwhile, for those who have successfully implemented behavioral targeting capabilities, the payoff has been tremendous. Tim Vanderhook, chief executive officer of online media network Specific Media, claims that compared to targeting by category (e.g., "sports fans"), or by mere clickthrough rates, behavioral targeting has doubled marketing's efficiency. Acxiom's Howe says his firm has seen two to three times the return; one Acxiom user, Andrea Palmer, manager of interactive services at Baltimore-based advertising agency Siquis, estimates 30 percent to 50 percent lower costs of advertising for her client, Spirit Airlines.

And there are other drawbacks to having a relatively young presence in the industry: "One of the most important things about behavioral targeting right now is that it's really ill-defined," Greene says, especially in terms of execution.

Much BT is highly dependent on the data that consumers provide through their Web activity. Historically, explains Specific Media's Vanderhook, companies that delivered adware—advertising-supported software—were the ones most often executing behavioral targeting. Every site a consumer visited was logged, triggering pop-up advertisements bundled within the adware. Not surprisingly, consumers became increasingly frustrated being interrupted by pop-up ads, marking their inevitable demise as a medium.

Limits on Behavioral Targeting

Today, marketers have access to both customer identity (IP [Internet protocol] address) and customer personality (online behavior). Now, BT often relies on HTTP cookies—small pieces of data used to track and maintain the online actions of a user, such as sites visited and even items stored in an electronic shopping cart. "A company is only as good at behavioral targeting as the amount of data [it has] access to," Vanderhook observes. So while the cookie history is in place, potentially relevant ads can be delivered, but once it is erased—or if the customer tries to access the same site from a different computer—"it's like a brand new person," he says.

Tools like cookies, however, have been subject to debate because of privacy concerns. To reassure wary marketers and their consumers, Howe explains that the concept of targeting "individuals" is actually a misnomer. Although behavioral targeting is significantly more relevant, it's not quite the Big Brother consumers fear it is. Behaviors are entirely based on what is registered through the server and, at most, combined with household demographic information obtained through public records. Currently, Vanderhook says, "I could never make a [random] ad that says, 'Name, click here for travel ads.'" But as databases get larger and more personal information is stored on the Web, security issues may become more of a concern, he says—perhaps leading regulators to try to restrict the industry in the name of individual privacy. Draconian reforms could hamstring behavioral efforts and innovations.

Another pitfall of targeting based on IP information is the discrepancy of shared computers. "We can't identify if someone gets up and another sits down," says Palmer, the manager at Siquis. Still, she believes that public computers are a minor concern for most marketers; in fact, Palmer says, "the times are few and far between when that many people are swapping computers to the point where the advertising might be skewed."

Following Users' Search Topics

The more widely recognized tactic of behavioral targeting is tracking individual behavior and marketing based on a "rule set," or serving ads based on the recency and frequency of a specific search topic. When the software detects high viewing rates of travel sites, for example, this presumably indicates that a consumer is nearing the end of her researching cycle and entering into buying mode. At this point, Vanderhook says, that consumer will be hit with more travel ads offering deals related to her previous search history. Still, he notes, even this approach has differing tactics: targeting consumers based on Web site visited, keyword searched, keywords read within content, or actions on your own Web site (e.g., "home-page viewers," "product information viewers," or "shopping cart abandoned viewers").

Not everyone agrees this is the best method—after all, customers are rarely ever just interested in one thing, says Jack Jia, chief executive officer of Baynote, a provider of what the company calls on-demand recommendation technology. "Clicks are more of a function," he adds. "They're not a good indicator of what's useful. . . . That's why the number-one-used button [on a Web site] is the 'back' button."

Jia argues that tracking the individual based on historical behavior stereotypes the consumer into being an insular person with singular wants. In response, Vanderhook says that clicks do provide useful insight when monitored for frequency over a short period of time. "You're not going to accidentally click eight times," he says.

Though Jia certainly has a point, when it comes to tracking across sites, targeting based on recency and frequency seems to be the best bet for today's marketers. "[A consumer's] historical Web-surfing behavior is absolutely critical," Vanderhook says.

Perhaps, then, one of the main reasons so few marketers are jumping on the behavioral-targeting bandwagon is because BT often requires more behavioral data than is currently available, according to JupiterResearch's Greene. Products or services that require longer purchase cycles and deeper research are able to satiate that prerequisite. As Vanderhook

Building Trust Among Consumers

Technology gives advertisers new opportunities to reach consumers more efficiently. To realize the promise of behavioral marketing, the online ad industry must build trust among consumers who increasingly demand more disclosure about what is being tracked on their computers and why. This is doable since behavioral marketing does not require the use of any personally identifiable information. However, the risks that concern consumers, such as identity theft and misuse of personal information, must be disassociated from behavioral marketing through PR [public relations] efforts. Lastly, if marketers adopt the principles of providing more transparency and giving consumers adequate value for using their data, they can advance the cause for behavioral marketing.

Bruce Clay, "The Promise of Behavioral Targeting," August 24, 2006. www.searchengineguide.com.

mentions, shopping for cars takes an average of six weeks—plenty of time for marketers to dish out campaigns.

Persistent but Realistic Messages

To target customers with multiple existing interests, Vanderhook explains that ads will only appear once online behavior in a particular category picks up. In the case of discount carrier Spirit Airlines, a consumer may select a trip from New York to Fort Lauderdale but exit the site before purchasing. If she lands on another travel site within the same advertising network, she will be presented with a traditional banner ad from Spirit reading, for example, "Low fares from New York City," or "Low fares to Fort Lauderdale." When consumers do leave a site before completing a transaction, Vanderhook, for one, is not afraid to make sure the consumer knows what benefits your product can offer over the competitor's. "You hit them at the next site that they're at, the next site, then the next site—with different messaging to make sure they're truly understanding what you're offering," he says.

As much as behavioral targeting focuses on delivering "in the moment," marketers are advised to know when to throw in the towel. Palmer has frequency caps on her campaigns: After a certain number of campaigns or after a certain time period, ads will no longer be delivered to that user. Persistence has its limits and realistically, "we don't want to waste any more advertisement on that person," Palmer says. For marketers who are just beginning to test the waters, Vanderhook suggests first experimenting with "retargeting." More straightforward, cost-effective, and less intrusive, Vanderhook believes "it's the single most powerful form of targeting in terms of turning visitors into customers." When an individual leaves your site and then later appears on a general, non-brand-specific site, marketers can retarget by hitting her with the ads for the specific product again, even outside their ad network. . . .

The Overall Consumer Experience

Although behavioral targeting has yet to achieve mainstream adoption, experts have no doubt the rest of the industry isn't far behind. "Much like direct mail in the [1970s] . . . people started off slow—didn't know what they were doing, didn't know how to target," Howe recollects. Eventually, he says, people got progressively better, and he predicts the same pattern will unfold for behavioral targeting as marketers apply offline lessons to the online world.

As BT reaches higher levels of sophistication, Vanderhook believes the next steps will be focused on truly achieving the dream of creating that highly coveted 360-degree view of the consumer. By combining demographic information and behavioral targeting, marketers will be able to determine not just which campaign to deliver, but which specific creative materials. Vanderhook illustrates a scenario where marketers can, in real time, identify whether the user is an 18-year-old male who would rather see a Honda with a pretty girl on the ad, or a working mother who would respond better to a Lexus ad with family-oriented features.

Technology is working to ameliorate the age-old marketing dilemma. As Howe states bluntly, "Stop bombarding your clients with crap." When it comes to customer relationship management, he says, "We do ourselves a disservice by basically burning out the consumers because we don't know what they want." In an era supposedly marked by an empowered consumer, marketers are being put to the test: Do it right or don't do it at all. But Howe seems confident that marketing's role in the overall consumer experience is here to stay: "We're going to evolve more, and more money's going to be spent on technology that offers consumers a better indication of a product or service that is aligned with their desires, wants, and needs."

> *"There are a number of legitimate business reasons for an employer to monitor employees' activity over the network."*

Employee Monitoring Is Necessary

Chris Petersen

In the following viewpoint, Chris Petersen claims that monitoring employees online at the workplace is necessary to protect the interests of the company. Keeping track of activity on the Web and in e-mail can fend off sexual harassment and breaches of confidentiality as well as ensure productivity, the author contends. Employees do not have an expectation of privacy when using the company's network, Petersen continues, and employers should devise and enforce a code of conduct for computer usage and communications. Petersen is an editor for Schofield Media Group, a business-to-business media company.

As you read, consider the following questions:

1. In Petersen's view, how can employee Internet use affect the company's network?

Chris Petersen, "Who's Watching You? Internet Monitoring in the Workplace Is Not Only Common, It's Necessary," *US Business Review*, vol. 9, 2008, pp. 6–7. Copyright © 2008 Schofield Media Ltd. Reproduced by permission.

2. What are commonly blocked Web sites, as stated by Petersen?

3. According to Phil Gordon, when would an employer be at fault for monitoring employee e-mail?

It's natural to be curious. When it comes to how your employees' behavior at work is impacting your bottom line, it's downright necessary.

Beginning with the time clock, employers have always been keeping a close eye on their employees to make sure that their time at work is well-spent.

The introduction of the Internet into the workplace has made it easier to get work done faster and communicate more efficiently, but it also has introduced new ways for your employees to sabotage your business, whether intentionally or by accident.

A 2007 survey conducted by the American Management Association (AMA) found that a significant number of employers have fired employees for misuse of the Internet and e-mail during company time.

Nearly 30 percent of employers have fired someone for reasons including visiting Web sites with inappropriate content, sending personal e-mails or breaching confidentiality rules.

Experts in the workplace privacy field say that monitoring employee Internet and e-mail usage is more common than one might think.

More than two-thirds of companies monitor their employees' Internet connections, according to the AMA survey, and a little less than half monitor e-mail. Although the idea of monitoring your employees' communication may sound like something out of a George Orwell novel, experts say it is vitally important to protect your company, and employees legally have to accept it as a fact of life.

Dave Coverly, "Yeah, I'm wasting time on one of those social notworking sites, too . . ."
Speed Bump, December 14, 2009.

Protecting Your Company

Monitoring is important for a variety of reasons, according to
Dave Walton, a labor and employment attorney for Philadelphia firm Cozen O'Connor.

He says employers typically monitor employees' Internet
usage to protect against sexual harassment and other types of
litigation, to protect confidential information, and to gauge
productivity. Employee Internet usage also can cause a drain

on the company's resources by eating up bandwidth or opening the door to computer viruses.

Phil Gordon, attorney with San Francisco–based labor and employment firm Littler Mendelson, says employers learned the importance of keeping an eye on e-mail and the Internet through the very public flogging of Chevron Corp. in 1995.

The company settled a sexual harassment lawsuit brought by four employees for $2.2 million.

The employees said they had received inappropriate and sexually explicit messages through company e-mail. Gordon says this case and many others prove that monitoring e-mail and the Internet isn't just about being nosy.

"There are a number of legitimate business reasons for an employer to monitor employees' activity over the network," he says.

There are many options for employers when it comes to monitoring their employees' use of the Internet. These can range from passive systems such as installing software to more active methods such as using internal investigators.

"You have technology out there that allows you to track keystrokes," Walton says, which gives an employer the ability to backtrack through an employee's entire interaction with the Internet.

According to the AMA survey, 45 percent of employers track keystrokes and time spent at keyboards.

Sixty-five percent use software to block certain Web sites from being accessed from company computers—a 27 percent jump from a 2001 survey also conducted by the AMA.

Although sexually oriented Web sites were by far the most frequently blocked, game sites, shopping sites and social networking sites also were on the list of forbidden Web pages.

Expectations of Privacy

No matter how an employer watches its employees on the Internet, Gordon says the employees should expect it. "Employees should have no expectation of privacy when they are using their employer's electronic resources," he says.

Even though some employees might consider this an invasion of their privacy, legally, whatever they do on the company's network belongs to the company.

"What your employees should expect is the use of their employer's e-mail for their personal use means someone else is going to read it," Gordon says.

Where employers get into trouble, he adds, is when employers give employees the assumption that their e-mail is private. Walton cites a case in which a police officer was fired for allegedly sending lewd text messages from a cell phone provided to him by the department. The courts overturned the officer's termination because the department's policy was that personal use was all right as long as the officer paid for any overages.

Walton says only two states mandate that employers notify employees that their Internet and e-mail usage will be monitored—Delaware and Connecticut. However, given that many people assume their e-mail is their own property, he adds, employers should make their monitoring public knowledge, regardless.

Where is the line when it comes to monitoring employees' use of the Internet?

At what point does an employer stop protecting the interests of his or her business and become a snoop?

The explosion of social networking sites such as MySpace and Facebook mean people's lives are more public than ever, and the potential for the workplace to enter into this territory is great. How far can an employer go to make sure his or her business is represented well on the Internet?

"As far as off-site activity, that is a tougher question," Gordon says. "The proper distinction should be whether we're looking at information stored on a corporate server . . . or information stored on a third-party server."

Gordon explains companies should regularly and consistently monitor [their] own servers, but they should have justifiable cause to begin poking around their employees' personal sites, including blogs.

"It goes back to why you're doing it," Walton says. "Are you doing it because you can or is there a legitimate purpose behind it?"

In cases where employers believe they have reason to fire an employee based on what they post on a public Web site, Walton says they should remember that if a lawsuit is filed, juries are more likely to side with employees.

"By and large, your members of a jury are your average Jane and Joe," he says. "All employers must be aware of that."

Social Networking as a Tool

Complicating matters is the fact that many companies are beginning to use social networking sites as part of their business, including networking with customers or vendors.

Even though the opportunity for employees to misuse networking sites is increased, Gordon says it also provides for the chance to make the company's stance clear.

"I'm starting to see a trend of employers embracing social networking and blogging and using them as tools for internal discussion and internal collaboration," Gordon says.

"I would strongly advise any employers who are going to introduce that kind of communication platform into the workplace to implement a code of conduct that puts all participants on notice in terms of the rules of behavior."

> *"The commonly held assumption that employers have unfettered access to electronic communications in the workplace has been called into question."*

Employee Monitoring Can Violate Privacy

Bruce Gain

In the following viewpoint, Bruce Gain states that employers do not have an absolute right to monitor their employees' online usage and communications. With the spread of the Internet in the workplace, Gain maintains that the perceived need to monitor employees has dramatically increased and created a demand for surveillance tools. Furthermore, monitoring practices have not yet been standardized, resulting in legal and ethical dilemmas, the author says. In fact, he asserts that it is the burden of businesses and organizations to disclose auditing and surveillance policies to workers. Gain is a contributor to Processor, *a computer-business magazine.*

As you read, consider the following questions:

1. In Jeremy Gruber's opinion, what did the privacy case in Ontario, California, demonstrate?

Bruce Gain, "Employee Monitoring's Murky Waters: The Legality & Ethics of Surveillance Are Far from Cut & Dried," *Processor*, vol. 30, August 15, 2008, Copyright © 2008 Sandhills Publishing Company. All rights reserved. Reproduced by permission.

2. How do many administrators view employee monitoring, according to Gain?

3. How does Gain bolster his allegation that many employers access more employee information than necessary?

The commonly held assumption that employers have unfettered access to electronic communications in the workplace has been called into question. In a federal court in California, a judge issued a verdict in June [2008] that said it was illegal for an employer to read employees' personal pager messages.

The case revolved around a member of the police department in Ontario, Calif., using a work-issued pager. After the police officer's supervisor told his staff that their text messages would not be monitored, the messages were audited. The officer claimed that it was illegal for members of the police bureau's internal affairs department to read the police officers' text messages from a pager that a third-party vendor supplied. While some of the messages were not work-related and were even sexually explicit, the appeals court ruled that the police officer had a reasonable expectation of privacy and that the audit of the messages was unlawful.

A Case Challenges the Status Quo

"Employers, I think, were very complacent in assuming that they could do whatever they wanted as far as workplace monitoring goes," says Jeremy Gruber, legal director for The National Workrights Institute. "This case demonstrates that the law is still developing on workplace monitoring. Employers who have programs that are overly broad and invasive could at some point find themselves on the wrong side of the law."

Gruber continues, "Specifically, this case makes it clear that employers using third-party vendors to administer their monitoring program do not have the same protections that employers who use their own equipment for monitoring do.

A Morale Problem

Organizations would be better off not [monitoring on-line activity] if they're going to scrutinize their employees' every move. If it creates a morale problem (and it will if it's not handled properly) all of its value is diminished. It must be done for business purposes, and this must be communicated to the employees. Zero tolerance won't work here either, just like it doesn't work in any other situation. There must be discretion and objectivity. Do you really want to reprimand an employee for reading the day's headline news?

Kevin Beaver, interviewed by Mia Shopis,
Security News, *December 9, 2003.*

Also, employers who use third-party vendors can find themselves liable for invasion of privacy if they don't have proper disclosure and proper notice depending on how they use the systems."

Indeed, the ruling has challenged the status quo, says Adam Schran, chief executive and founder of Ascentive, which designs and markets employee monitoring software. "It did come as a total surprise," Schran says. "The legal situation is in flux, so you have to be in contact with your lawyers or the general counsel of the company to make sure you are doing it in the right way."

Employee monitoring has entered the realm of legally murky territory. This means qualified legal counsel to guide SMEs [small and medium enterprises] about what they can and cannot do has become more important than it was in the past.

The perceived need to monitor employees' communications has skyrocketed. Since employers first began to fret over how staffers could waste time, the explosion of ways to goof off at work has compounded demand for surveillance tools to keep an eye on workers' activities. According to Ascentive, employee monitoring, blocking, and filtering product sales have become a $300 million-a-year market since they were first introduced for mainstream applications more than a decade ago.

An Ethical Dilemma

Surveillance of employees' electronic communications also involves ethical issues admins [administrators] need to address, even if the monitoring is perfectly legal. Many admins may be uncomfortable with employee monitoring, especially when a company implements a heavy-handed policy and asks admins to use technology to closely monitor what employees write in their email messages or which Web sites they visit.

"I would tell my boss that it's unethical, in my opinion, to monitor employees if they have not signed an agreement that fully sets their expectations about the monitoring. If the boss wanted to do the monitoring, we could send out a form to all employees that they would all sign and return before any monitoring begins," says John Matzek, co-chief executive officer of Logic IT Consulting. "I would also expect the boss and the CEO [chief executive officer] to sign the form. Employee morale is critical to the success of a business, and covert monitoring could have a huge impact on morale."

The general public is also becoming more aware of how admins are often privy to the contents of employees' email and other electronic communications. Cyber-Ark, a provider of digital vault and privileged identity management technology, recently caused a stir when it revealed that 47% of 300 senior IT [information technology] professionals surveyed said they had "accessed information that was not relevant to their role."

"As an administrator, I will often need to fix or maintain the email system," Matzek says. "I agree to keep client information confidential, but I will often need to log in as a user to troubleshoot their email issues or make sure things are working after maintenance."

Policy Matters

General industry-standard guidelines for employee monitoring have not been established; it is up to individual enterprises to set their own policies, while the IT department must determine how it does monitoring.

"Employee monitoring is fairly common in policy but varied in practice," says Michael Rasmussen, president of Corporate Integrity. "Most organizations have policies in place to establish that employees should not have an expectation of privacy and that the corporation retains rights to monitor communications. However, the practice is quite varied."

Still, there are certain policies all enterprises should follow, Rasmussen says. "Organizations that are going to pursue monitoring need to have a policy in place that states that there is no expectation of employee privacy and that the organization reserves the right to monitor communication," he notes. "Monitoring also has to be done for a legitimate purpose and cannot be done in a way that discriminates against an individual."

Periodical Bibliography

The following articles have been selected to supplement the diverse views presented in this chapter.

Sam Barrett — "Monitoring Raises Privacy Issues," *Employee Benefits*, May 2008.

Laurie Burkett — "Consumer Privacy: Who Cares? Companies Will Soon Find Out," *Forbes*, November 18, 2009.

Marcia Clemmitt — "Privacy in Peril: Smile, Your Employer May Be Watching," *CQ Researcher*, November 17, 2006.

Jay Cline — "Opinion: Will the Smart Grid Protect Consumer Privacy?" *Computerworld*, November 17, 2009.

Michael Dobbs — "Schools and Military Face Off," *Washington Post*, June 19, 2005.

Susan Essoyan — "Recruiter Misled Students, a Navy Investigation Finds," *Honolulu Star-Bulletin*, August 31, 2009.

Adrian Miedema and Andy Pushalik — "How, and When, Employers Should Monitor Employees," *Canadian HR Reporter*, November 2, 2009.

Lee C. Milstein — "Avoiding Legal Pitfalls on User-Generated Content Sites," *Journal of Internet Law*, September 2007.

Brittany Petersen — "Employee Monitoring: It's Not Paranoia—You Really Are Being Watched!" *PC Magazine*, May 26, 2008.

Megan Tady — "The Military's Stealth Test," *In These Times*, December 7, 2007.

Frank Watson — "Behavioral Targeting: Profiling or Perfecting User Experience," *Search Engine Watch*, March 13, 2009.

For Further Discussion

Chapter 1

1. John Yoo contends that critics exaggerate the Patriot Act's threats to privacy. Are the *Los Angeles Times*'s claims exaggerated in your view? Cite from the texts to support your response.

2. Jayson P. Ahern insists that suspicionless searches of laptops have been found constitutional by the courts in numerous cases. In your opinion, how persuasive is Ahern's position? Explain your answer.

3. Sandra Kay Miller proposes that a unified identification system would make Americans safer. Becky Akers, on the other hand, maintains that it would give the government more intrusive access to their personal information. In your view, who makes the more compelling argument? Use examples from the viewpoints to support your answer.

Chapter 2

1. Simson Garfinkel says that abstinence from everyday technological activity cannot fully protect privacy. Could you better protect your own privacy by not using the Internet and avoiding computers and electronic transactions? Why or why not?

2. Glen W. Fewkes says that emerging surveillance technologies may infringe on privacy in unprecedented ways. Does J. Richard Gray successfully respond to this issue? Use examples from the viewpoints to support your response.

3. Todd Lewan argues that information on electronic passports can be read or intercepted in several ways. Does *Security* convince you that these documents are secure from such attacks? Why or why not?

Chapter 3

1. Karen J. Maschke describes a backdoor method of obtaining DNA from suspects by following them secretly and collecting samples. In your opinion, can this practice be justified? Why or why not?

2. Jennifer Kern, Fatema Gunja, Alexandra Cox, Marsha Rosenbaum, Judith Appel, and Anjuli Verma assert that drug testing would deter students from participating in extracurricular activities. Would you take a drug test to play sports or be a member of the band or a school club? Cite from the viewpoints to explain your response.

Chapter 4

1. Jody Feder describes two ways in which parents are notified when military recruiters request student contact information. In your view, are these notices adequate? Use examples from the viewpoint to explain your response.

2. Jessica Tsai claims that it is a misperception that marketers target an individual on the Internet. Does Pamela Jones Harbour uphold this supposed misperception? Cite from the texts to support your answer.

3. Chris Petersen and Bruce Gain cite the case in which a police officer's termination over inappropriate texting on a mobile device was overturned in court because the employer's policies did not prohibit personal use. Are Petersen's and Gain's positions on the case similar or different? Use examples from the viewpoints to explain your response.

Organizations to Contact

The editors have compiled the following list of organizations concerned with the issues debated in this book. The descriptions are derived from materials provided by the organizations. All have publications or information available for interested readers. The list was compiled on the date of publication of the present volume; the information provided here may change. Be aware that many organizations take several weeks or longer to respond to inquiries, so allow as much time as possible.

American Civil Liberties Union (ACLU)
125 Broad St., 18th Fl., New York, NY   10004-2400
(212) 549-2500
e-mail: aclu@aclu.org
Web site: www.aclu.org

The ACLU is a national organization that works to defend civil rights as guaranteed in the U.S. Constitution. It publishes various materials on civil liberties, including the national newsletter *Civil Liberties*, and a set of handbooks on individual rights. "Enforcing Privacy: Building American Institutions to Protect Privacy in the Face of New Technology and Government Powers" and "Lifestyle Discrimination in the Workplace: Your Right to Privacy Under Attack" are two of its articles.

Brookings Institution
1775 Massachusetts Ave. NW, Washington, DC   20036
(202) 797-6000
Web site: www.brookings.edu

The Brookings Institution, founded in 1927, is a think tank that conducts research and education in foreign policy, economics, government, and the social sciences. In 2001, it began America's Response to Terrorism, a project that provides briefings and analysis to the public and which is featured on the center's Web site. Other publications include the quarterly *Brookings Review*, periodic *Policy Briefs*, and books such as *Power Play: The Bush Presidency and the Constitution*.

CATO Institute

1000 Massachusetts Ave. NW, Washington, DC   20001-5403
(202) 842-0200 • fax: (202) 842-3490
Web site: www.cato.org

CATO is a nonpartisan public policy research foundation dedicated to limiting the role of government and protecting individual liberties. It publishes the quarterly magazine *Regulation*, the bimonthly *Cato Policy Report*, and numerous policy papers and articles. *Identity Crisis: How Identification Is Overused and Misunderstood* and "Government-Run Cyber Security? No, Thanks" are among its books and articles on privacy and security.

Electronic Frontier Foundation (EFF)

454 Shotwell St., San Francisco, CA   94110-1914
(415) 436-9333
e-mail: information@eff.org
Web site: www.eff.org

EFF is an organization that aims to promote a better understanding of telecommunications issues. It fosters awareness of civil liberties issues arising from advancements in computer-based communications media and supports litigation to preserve, protect, and extend First Amendment rights in computing and telecommunications technologies. EFF's publications include the electronic newsletter *EFFector Online* and white papers such as "The Clicks That Bind: Ways Users 'Agree' to Online Terms of Service" and "On Locational Privacy, and How to Avoid Losing It Forever."

Electronic Privacy Information Center (EPIC)

1718 Connecticut Ave. NW, Suite 200, Washington, DC   20009
(202) 483-1140 • fax: (202) 483-1248
Web site: www.epic.org

As an advocate of the public's right to electronic privacy, EPIC sponsors educational and research programs, compiles statistics, and conducts litigation pertaining to privacy and other civil liberties. Its publications include the biweekly electronic newsletter *EPIC Alert* and its *EPIC Privacy Report Card.*

Federal Aviation Administration (FAA)
800 Independence Ave. SW, Washington, DC   20591
(866) TELL-FAA (835-5322)
Web site: www.faa.gov

The Federal Aviation Administration is the component of the U.S. Department of Transportation whose primary responsibility is the safety of civil aviation. The FAA's major functions include regulating civil aviation to promote safety and fulfill the requirements of national defense. Its International Flight Information Manual page contains links to terrorism-related information.

Federal Bureau of Investigation (FBI)
J. Edgar Hoover Bldg., 935 Pennsylvania Ave. NW, Room 7972
Washington, DC   20535
(202) 324-3000
Web site: www.fbi.gov

The FBI, the principal investigative arm of the U.S. Department of Justice, investigates specific crimes assigned to it and provides other law enforcement agencies with cooperative services, such as fingerprint identification, laboratory examinations, and police training. The mission of the FBI is to uphold the law through the investigation of violations of federal criminal law and to protect the United States from foreign intelligence and terrorist activities in a manner that is faithful to the U.S. Constitution. Press releases, congressional statements, and major speeches are available on the agency's Web site.

Federal Trade Commission (FTC)
600 Pennsylvania Ave. NW, Washington, DC   20580
(202) 326-2222
Web site: www.ftc.gov

The Federal Trade Commission works to ensure that the nation's markets are vigorous, efficient and free of restrictions that harm consumers. The FTC enforces federal consumer protection laws that prevent fraud, deception, and unfair business practices and combats identity theft, Internet scams, and telemarketing fraud. Publications posted on the FTC Web site offer consumer information concerning telemarketing, credit cards, and identity theft.

The Heritage Foundation

214 Massachusetts Ave. NE, Washington, DC   20002-4999
(202) 546-4400 • fax: (202) 546-8328
e-mail: info@heritage.org
Web site: www.heritage.org

The Heritage Foundation is a conservative public policy research institute that supports the principles of free enterprise and limited government in individual and business matters. Its many publications include the Backgrounder series of position papers, including papers concerning terrorism, privacy rights, and constitutional issues.

National Security Agency (NSA)

9800 Savage Rd., Suite 6248, Fort Meade, MD   20755-6248
(301) 688-6524
e-mail: nsapao@nsa.gov
Web site: www.nsa.gov

The National Security Agency coordinates, directs, and performs activities that protect American information systems and produce foreign intelligence information. The NSA employs satellites to collect data from telephones and computers, aiding in the fight against terrorism. Speeches, briefings, and reports are available on its Web site.

National Workrights Institute

166 Wall St., Princeton, NJ   08540
(609) 683-0313

e-mail: info@workrights.org
Web site: www.workrights.org

The National Workrights Institute was founded in January 2000 by the former staff of the American Civil Liberties Union's National Taskforce on Civil Liberties in the Workplace. The institute's goal is to improve the legal protection of human rights in the workplace and to see that employment laws are adequately enforced and strengthened. The institute publishes annual reports and provides information for articles in newspapers, national magazines, and television shows.

Office of the Privacy Commissioner of Canada

112 Kent St., Place de Ville, Tower B, Third Fl.
Ottawa, ON   K1A 1H3
   Canada
(800) 282-1376 • fax: (613) 947-6850
Web site: www.priv.gc.ca

An advocate for the privacy rights of Canadians, the privacy commissioner investigates complaints from individuals with respect to the federal laws; reports on the information-handling practices of the public and private sectors; conducts audits; and promotes awareness of privacy issues. The privacy commissioner's Web site details Canada's privacy legislation, provides privacy impact assessments, and offers various fact sheets. Its resource page contains such publications as the office's annual reports to Parliament, official speeches, and privacy rights guidelines for businesses and individuals.

Privacy Rights Clearinghouse (PRC)

3100 Fifth Ave., Suite B, San Diego, CA   92103
(619) 298-3396 • fax: (619) 298-5681
Web site: www.privacyrights.org

The Privacy Rights Clearinghouse is a nonprofit consumer organization with a two-part mission—to provide consumer information and advocate for consumer privacy. The group raises awareness of how technology affects personal privacy, empowers consumers to take action to control their own personal information by providing practical tips on privacy protection, responds to privacy-related complaints from consumers, and reports this information. Its Web site provides transcripts of PRC speeches and testimony, stories of consumer experiences, and numerous fact sheets.

Bibliography of Books

Katherine   *The Spychips Threat: Why Christians*
Albrecht and   *Should Resist RFID and Electronic*
Liz McIntyre   *Surveillance.* Nashville: Nelson
                    Current, 2006.

Collin J. Bennett   *The Privacy Advocates: Resisting the*
                    Spread of Surveillance. Cambridge,
                    MA: MIT Press, 2008.

Collin J. Bennett   *Playing the Identity Card:*
and David Lyon   *Surveillance, Security, and*
                    Identification in Global Perspective.
                    New York: Routledge, 2008.

Anupam Chander,   *Securing Privacy in the Internet Age.*
Lauren Gelman,   Stanford, CA: Stanford Law Books,
and Margaret   2008.
Jane Radin, eds.

Michael Chertoff   *Homeland Security: Assessing the First*
                    Five Years. Philadelphia: University of
                    Pennsylvania Press, 2009.

Whitfield Diffie   *Privacy on the Line: The Politics of*
and Susan   *Wiretapping and Encryption.* 2nd ed.
Landau   Cambridge, MA: MIT Press, 2007.

Laura K.   *The Cost of Counterterrorism: Power,*
Donohue   *Politics, and Liberty.* New York:
                    Cambridge University Press, 2008.

W.D. Edmiston   *Why Parents Should Fear MySpace.*
                    Longwood, FL: Xulon Press, 2007.

Jon Erickson   *Hacking: The Art of Exploitation..* 2nd ed. San Francisco: No Starch Press, 2008.

Amy L. Fairchild, Ronald Bayer, James Colgrove   *Searching Eyes: Privacy, the State, and Disease Surveillance in America.* Berkeley and Los Angeles: University of California Press, 2007.

Elizabeth Price Foley   *Liberty for All: Reclaiming Individual Privacy in a New Era of Public Morality.* New Haven, CT: Yale University Press, 2006.

Frederick S. Lane   *American Privacy: The 400-Year History of Our Most Contested Right.* Boston: Beacon, 2009.

Jay Liebowitz   *Social Networking: The Essence of Innovation.* Lanham, MD: Rowman & Littlefield, 2007.

Duncan Long   *Protect Your Privacy: How to Protect Your Identity as Well as Your Financial, Personal, and Computer Records in an Age of Constant Surveillance.* Guilford, CT: Lyons Press, 2007.

Thomas N. McInnis   *The Evolution of the Fourth Amendment.* Lanham, MD: Lexington Books, 2009.

Jon L. Mills   *Privacy: The Lost Right.* New York: Oxford University Press, 2008.

James B. Rule   *Privacy in Peril: How We Are Sacrificing a Fundamental Right in Exchange for Security and Convenience.* New York: Oxford University Press, 2007.

Christopher Slobogin   *Privacy at Risk: The New Government Surveillance and the Fourth Amendment.* Chicago: University of Chicago Press, 2008.

Janet E. Smith   *The Right to Privacy.* Ft. Collins, CO: Ignatius Press, 2008.

Wolfgang Sofsky   *Privacy: A Manifesto.* Princeton, NJ: Princeton University Press, 2007.

Daniel J. Solove   *The Future of Reputation: Gossip, Rumor, and Privacy on the Internet.* Ann Arbor, MI: Caravan Books, 2007.

Daniel J. Solove   *Understanding Privacy.* Cambridge, MA: Harvard University Press, 2008.

John T. Soma and Stephen D. Rynerson   *Privacy Law in a Nutshell.* St. Paul, MN: Thomson/West, 2008.

Jeannie Suk   *At Home in the Law: How the Domestic Violence Revolution Is Transforming Privacy.* New Haven, CT: Yale University Press, 2009.

Index

A

Absolutist position of civil libertarians, 24–26

AccuTracking service, 67

ActivIdentity, Inc., 50

Aerial photography, 108

Ahern, Jayson P., 39–47

Airport security, 32–38, 110

Akers, Becky, 54–64

Al-Qaeda terrorist group, 2, 19
   See also 9/11/2001 terrorist attack

Alcoholics Anonymous (AA), 103

Alexa Web service firm, 76

Alien and Sedition Acts (1798), 22

Amazon.com, 81

American Association of Motor Vehicle Administrators, 58

American Civil Liberties Union (ACLU)
   Facebook opinion, 15
   symbolic resolution encouragement, 23
   video surveillance opinions, 110
   vs. REAL ID Act, 50, 57

American Constitution Society for Law and Policy, 145

American Student List (ASL), 179–180

Anderson, Thomas, 25

Annenberg School for Communication (University of Pennsylvania), 101

Appel, Judith, 157–165

Armed Services Vocational Aptitude Battery (ASVAB), 181

Arms Export Control Act (AECA), 42

Arnold, Michael, 40

Association of Corporate Travel Executives, 122

ASVAB Career Exploration Program, 181

ATM (automated teller machine) transactions, 89, 92

AutoAdmit online message board, 74

B

Backscatter X-ray technology, 110–111

Banking online, 81

Bankston, Kevin, 15–16

Bill of Rights, 22

Biometric chip tracking device, 56, 64

Black Hat security firm, 115

Blogging, 93–94

Blown to Bits: Your Life, Liberty and Happiness After the Digital Explosion (Leeden & Lewis), 85

Board of Education of Pottawatomie County v. Earls, 155, 161

Boston Globe (newspaper), 51

Brandeis, Louis, 72–73

Brandewie, Rob, 50–51

Burlington (VT) *Free Press,* 25

Bush, George W., 22, 26, 28

Business Travel Coalition, 122

223

YA 323.448 P93
Privacy :

FEB 2 4 2011